Liquid
Risks

The New Challenges to Global Security

Smart Risk Consulting

Risks | Forecasting | Markets | Publishing

Liquid
Risks

The New Challenges to Global Security

Reality is no longer fixed and unchanging. Instead, it appears as a constantly flowing and evolving phenomenon where nothing remains static for too long. It is a continuous process of transformation that renders previous states obsolete and makes future developments unpredictable.

Alberto Ray

Smart Risk Consulting
Risks | Forecasting | Markets | Publishing

Liquid Risks
The new challenges to global security
Alberto Ray
Edited by Smart Risk Consulting LLC
Tampa Florida, 34638 - USA

Translation: Lorenzo Dávalos
Art Direction: Alejandro C. Pacheco
Graphic Design: Alejandro C. Pacheco
Cover: Alejandro C. Pacheco and Alberto Ray
Editing: Florantonia Singer
and Lorenzo Dávalos
Prologue: Luís Emilio Bruni
Printing Kindle Direct Publishing
Printed in the USA
ISBN 979-8-218-44838-7
Tampa, Florida -
© Alberto Ray- 2024
Contact: alberto@albertoray.com
X: @seguritips

To the Venezuelan migrants, immense fractional
expression of my nation.

"Today, culture does not consist of prohibitions but of offers; it does not consist of norms but of proposals. Today, culture is concerned with offering temptations and establishing attractions, with seduction and lures instead of regulations, with public relations instead of police supervision: producing, sowing, and planting new desires and needs instead of imposing duty.

Zygmunt Bauman

"Faced with all these dangers, we must seek a more open, more global, and complex way of thinking. We need to reject dogmatism, the hardening of our ideas, and the refusal to contrast them with reality. We need to abandon a closed rationalism that cannot grasp what might be beyond conventional thinking and instead (we should) embrace an open rationalism that knows its limitations. We have to constantly fight to avoid believing in those illusions that could take on the solidity of a belief system. In this global world, we face the challenge of global thinking, which is the challenge of complex thinking. We are living the beginning of a beginning."

Edgar Morin

Table of Contents

When submerged in a liquid, the most efficient way to move is not by applying power but rather by moving with fluid movements, thus conferring the risk analyst the same fluidity of the liquid in which he is immersed.

Prologue

It is common sense that times change, and no era is identical to the previous one. What could be debatable is whether the speed of change has always been more or less constant or if the perception of acceleration that overwhelms us is an unprecedented phenomenon. This perception, which Alberto refers to in his book as accelerationism (with the consequent addiction to change that it gives rise to), could be considered just a perception or, on the contrary, it could be an ontological fact determined by the incremental hyper-connectivity of communication and human activities, which gives rise to increasingly complex causal concatenations. In this liquid world, Alberto identifies a new category of risks: liquid risks.

At first glance, the array of concepts introduced in this book may seem overwhelming. Terms such as accelerationism, takinesis, alternative truths, virtualization, the principle of invisibility, criminal peace, multiplexed beings, security, antifragility, and, above all, the central notions referring to the liquid: the liquid world, liquid organizations and their correlate, liquid risks, might appear unfamiliar. However, your understanding of these concepts is crucial, as it will enable you to navigate the complexities of the liquid world.

Alberto's strategy is not to introduce a glossary but to define and interconnect these terms contextually. Thus, the book presents its terminology iteratively as the concepts are applied to particular situations and cases. In this way, the reader can become familiar with a series of concepts that may seem foreign in the beginning, but as the book progresses, the terms gain meaning and relevance. The reader's patience will be rewarded with an innovative and cohesive perspective on the risks and complexities of today's world.

One of the sources of inspiration in Alberto's work is the thesis of the German sociologist Ulrich Beck. Indeed, Beck accurately defined three of the major characteristics of what are here identified as liquid risks. First, what makes these risks novel is their anthropogenic origin. Although many of them are introduced by the techno-scientific processes of modernization, in the liquid world portrayed by Alberto, not all are an exclusive by-product of these processes. Nevertheless, they are supported and magnified by the complexity of said developments (for example, transnational criminal activities in the digital world). Second, these risks constitute cross-border or transnational risks and are, therefore, difficult to contain. They are not limited to their places of origin, and their effects can emerge long afterward. So, it is challenging to determine the individual (or local) causes and responsibilities. Finally, these risks are invisible to the human eye, and therefore, to be able to evaluate them, one is bound to depend on instruments, technologies, and specialized scientific knowledge. This last characteristic, Beck warned, would give rise to deep states of collective anxiety, controversial uncertainties, and political manipulations of scientific knowledge and information. For example, let us consider all the levels and sources of uncertainty that pervaded an unprecedented global phenomenon such as the SARS-CoV-2 pandemic: uncertainty regarding its origin, uncertainty regarding the development of its epidemiological behavior, uncertainty regarding the pathological mechanisms, uncertainty regarding the human immunological response, uncertainty regarding its treatment, as well as the preferred preventive and prophylactic methods; uncertainty regarding the effectiveness and safety of vaccines; and, in all its complexity, uncertainty regarding the management of information about all these uncertainties themselves. This latter uncertainty being highly susceptible to political, economic, and geostrategic conditioning.

Information management in contemporary digital culture also represents an example of a highly complex liquid risk. It is a risk created by contemporary technoscientific processes, with global consequences that are impossible to elucidate in their spatiotemporal origins. Just like the pandemic, the risks of digitization remain indiscernible to the average citizen who struggles to assess the dangers of privacy infringement, the reliability of information manipulated or filtered by algorithms, or the misinformation propagated by technologies that obscure the boundaries between reality, falsehood, and fiction. Much like the pandemic, these sociocultural risks hinge on specialized techno-scientific expertise to unravel their origins, mitigate their harms, and understand their intricate causal connections with social, political, economic, and geostrategic processes.

One of the characteristics of complex systems is that emergent effects are exponentially amplified across the different levels of complexity of the system as a whole. The interaction between factors at different levels adds up to the intrinsic complexity of each of them. In that perspective, as an example, let us take an additional step forward and combine the uncertainties inherent to the liquid risks of a pandemic with those of information management in contemporary digital culture to get an idea of the levels and type of complexity that modern citizens and organizations are facing today.

Liquid risks exacerbate the growing crisis of credibility in democratic institutions, which in turn show severe signs of deterioration in their daily operations, being rendered ineffective in guaranteeing the freedoms and rights of citizens. Alberto elaborates eloquent examples of how the proliferation of liquid risks feeds back into the interplay between politics, transnational economic interests, and organized crime: "... what constitutes a risk is the acceleration of the gap between the capabilities of criminal networks to create gray zones, aimed at producing harm, and the response of institutional and judicial forces to neutralize them" In these gray areas, another liquid risk emerges in full development: the blurring of the boundaries between organized crime, entrepreneurs, financiers, consortia, holdings corporations, foundations, States, non-governmental organizations, and even multilateral organizations that include States of dubious legitimacy and transparency. From there, the crisis of trust in institutions (both national and international) arises, opening the doors to potential fractures in the social cohesion of nations and societies. In this context, the prevailing narratives also liquefy, blurring the borders between what is real and what is delusive, reality and fiction, simulacrum and hyperreality. The fabrication of narratives and realities thus becomes a privileged instrument for systemic corruption and the erosion of accountability in democratic societies, generating the collective anxiety states that Beck referred to.

Presciently, Beck also warned that, given the complexity and levels of uncertainty at stake, science could not expect to keep on holding a monopoly on rationality, and politicians could not appeal to it as an indisputable legitimizing factor for their own political, economic, or geostrategic agendas. First, science is not a uniform, monolithic entity; on the contrary, science is a complex sociocultural process built on perspectives, agreements, consensuses, disputes, controversies, debates, and contrasting scientific philosophies. What generates credibility and trust in science is openness, discussion, absolute transparency, and academic freedom. This contrasts with the liquid risk that a global ideology for control and discrimination could arise in our times based on a slogan like 'trust the science.

Beck maintained that science's allegation of being able to investigate the dangerousness of these risks was based exclusively on a framework of probabilistic statements. When faced with uncertainties or risks of this nature and magnitude, it is pertinent to ask ourselves what type of uncertainties our probabilistic and statistical models are helping us avoid: do they help us prevent our ignorance and lack of information about the events under evaluation? Or are they allowing us to circumvent the indeterminacy intrinsic to the process? In considering liquid risks, we are called to humbly assume that ontological indeterminacy plays a more fundamental role in our probabilistic models than calculating our ignorance about the system, which would be theoretically minimized with more and better information. In liquid risks, both sources of uncertainty, the reducible (epistemological) and the irreducible (ontological), must be considered and elaborated.

Beck's conclusion at the time was that just as social rationality without scientific rationality was a blind rationality, scientific rationality without social rationality would be an empty rationality. It will always be necessary to assume an ethical point of view to discuss these risks meaningfully. It is usually believed and thought that the ethical issue in science and technology lies essentially in the way in which science is used, misused, or not used sufficiently or equitably. But it is always assumed that there is only one model of science and that its practice is fully adequate to elucidate and resolve new risks, many of which paradoxically originate in the practice of science itself (for example, the risks linked to experimentation with gain of function in viruses or bacteria). The possibility that science itself may need changes towards less reductionist perspectives and more awareness of the inherent limits posed by complexity and its causal concatenations seems to be off the radar of those who supported this new trust the science movement, which, rather than on a scientific argument, was supported on an argument from authority.

In a lucid and seminal essay from 1972, anthropologist and co-founder of cybernetics Gregory Bateson identified three fundamental causes of what he called the roots of the ecological crisis. This crisis was epistemological and cultural for him. Those three causes would be mutually reinforcing each other in three overlapping rings of positive feedback: i) population growth, ii) technological innovation, and iii) our cultural pathologies, which Bateson characterized with the Greek notion of hubris, usually understood as a combination of arrogance and overconfidence. For obvious ethical reasons, Bateson disregarded certain contemporary emerging trends that deem population control, and in some radical cases even depopulation of the planet, as effective strategies for mitigating the ecological crisis. Instead, he saw it as a priority to intervene in the overlap of the exponential technological development with the scientific hubris of modern positivism, which in turn is intertwined with economic determinism and thousands of cultural details, which today are tautologically instilled in our culture to drive humanity towards a technocratic *eudaimonia* in which Science would serve as a legitimizing principle in the hands of *de facto* powers, and technology would become its executing arm.

In 1984, the philosopher Han Jonas, in his essential work The Imperative of Responsibility: In Search of an Ethics for the Technological Age, characterized the blind cult of innovation (scientific and technological) as a perspective of nihilistic freedom that exempted itself from the need for any justification, and therefore claiming that what it constituted, truly, was a profession of irresponsibility. The phenomenon of accelerationism, developed by Alberto in the book, is directly related to the process of technological convergence that Bateson described as positive feedback between different types of disruptive technologies. An example of this may be what, in recent decades, has been called the NBIC convergence between nanotechnologies, biotechnologies, information technologies, and cognitive sciences. This convergence will increasingly play a central role in emerging new liquid risks, their volatility, and their camouflaging in different interconnected contexts. The democratic societies will be subjected to grueling tests to demonstrate their capacity and relevance in preserving the historical achievements of humanity in terms of human rights, individual guarantees, and even universally established bioethical principles such as the principle of autonomy. This is where transparency and accountability in democratic societies play a fundamental role. Can the politicians in these societies make explicit their mid- and long-term visions on these inalienable rights and guarantees? Are the citizens of these societies capable of demanding that their politicians and rulers make their visions on those rights and guarantees explicit?

Despite the blind trust in scientific positivism (where big data and artificial intelligence can be seen as a contemporary expression of the ontological determinism of Laplace's demon), risk management in the way it has been traditionally established in technical institutions and legal systems has shown its collapse, just as Ulrich Beck predicted at the time. Risks can no longer be quantified in terms of the probabilities of their occurrence without considering the magnitude and complexity of their nature, as foreseen by Hans Jonas. Risks that are not scientifically quantifiable and, because of that, excluded from institutional legal frameworks can no longer be ignored.

Alberto invites us to consider, through a network of interconnected examples, that our knowledge and understanding of liquid risks do not guarantee our ability to predict them. Awareness of these risks and their context does not ensure a possible intervention to minimize or control them. However, the development of this awareness is vital to transform our state of alert into an adaptive aikido movement that projects the risk in the same way that the martial artist projects his adversary: "Safety would no longer only be a process that reduces the vulnerabilities of an object or an environment, but by building full awareness of the risk, it turns the subject into the leading actor and active analyst of the dangers that surround him, allowing him to predictably decide a route to dismantle those risks, even before they become evident."

In Alberto's perspective, "uncertainty is the central link in the chain of formation of liquid risks." Therefore, it is on managing uncertainty that we must focus our efforts. However, as the book emphasizes, new complexities and liquid risks leave us in the wrong position regarding predictions. For this reason, rather than predicting all adverse scenarios to get a menu of responses for each one, the approach would focus on new skills to develop an awareness of risk liquidity and thus create a kind of situational readiness that allows us to react adaptively in real-time. In the case of complex processes, as previously mentioned, some uncertainties are reducible, for example, with more and better information, better sources of intelligence, better predictive methods and systems, and better models with more powerful computational capacities (that is, epistemological uncertainties). But we would dare to affirm that there are ontological uncertainties in liquid risks, that is, uncertainties intrinsic to the complexity, chaos, and emergent properties inherent to these risks. Therefore, notwithstanding how much information is gathered about an issue deemed the source of a specific risk, a residual amount will always remain. This type of "liquid" uncertainty – to follow the book's main thread– requires the kind of jujitsu or aikido response recommended by Alberto, that is, the creation of awareness and readiness necessary for adaptability and response in real-time.

Alberto states, "There is no more complicated challenge than predicting the future. However, we have to assume that the past is no longer a sufficient reference to face the magnitude and quality of threats that this new dynamic of the liquid brings with it, even more so when the future accelerates..." In other words, you cannot have a deterministic approach to liquid risks; even a stochastic approach would find its limits. Probabilistic modeling and prediction systems were developed expressly to circumvent the observer's ignorance of detailed events that were assumed to be amenable to a classical deterministic view. Similar models were developed for inherently stochastic situations.

Since the advent of the complexity sciences, ontological indeterminacy has been given increasing credence as the object of statistical consideration over ignorance or lack of information about the system. In other words, we went from probabilities that were a function of our ignorance or lack of information about the system or process in question to probabilities that now reflect an indeterminacy inherent to the process and related to the events' ontological nature. Such is the case of liquid risks: "Certainties, therefore, are built on frames of reference and perceptions and not only on facts... not all certainties are tangible and, in many cases, their opposite, uncertainty, is absolute". Failure to understand this characteristic of liquid risks would lead us to mistakenly interpret any defect in our predictive model as a gap in our current knowledge, with the erroneous presumption that more knowledge and more information will reduce uncertainties, increase our control capacity, and allow us to remedy the problems of the past.

Disciplines such as Aikido, Judo, and Jiu Jitsu frequently use water metaphorically. Given their fluidity, liquid risks are highly insidious. That is why they demand an equally fluid response. When submerged in a liquid, the most efficient way to move is not by applying power but rather by moving with fluid movements, thus conferring the risk analyst the same fluidity of the liquid in which he is immersed. We can dodge and get out of the target but not run away. In Aikido, you seek to flow with your opponent. There is never a head-on collision. There are no hard surfaces to crash into. The adversary is induced to follow his own trajectory until a slight balance disruption causes him to collapse to the ground, where he can be neutralized.

We live in exceptional times. Maybe all times are exceptional. But indeed, not all have been liquid in the connotation presented in this book. If current history continues, the world's liquidity and risks will increase. But it is not necessary for it to be like that. Not if we raise awareness of the risk and the existence of alternative trajectories. Just as Alberto advocates for the need to dismantle the sense of inevitability of catastrophic narratives, I think it is equally essential to dismantle the sense of inevitability of the Baconian dream narratives of technological convergence, which the philosopher Hans Jonas warned us about. This positivist dream not only promises the illusion of the resolution of all emerging risks - be they military, biosecurity, health, ecological, food security, crime, or social, political, and cultural chaos - but also promises a technological nirvana, whose postulate of inevitability makes it intrinsically totalitarian, mutilating and denying of the inalienable right to simply be human.

Good reading.
Luis E. Bruni
Copenhagen, March 2024

About Luis E. Bruni

With a multidisciplinary international training, Luis Emilio Bruni is an environmental engineer graduated from Penn State University, with a master's degree in international and global relations from the Central University of Venezuela, and a PhD in biosemiotics and theory of science at the Institute of Molecular Biology of the University from Copenhagen, with extensive scientific production and interdisciplinary teaching experience. Since 2004 he has been developing his research at Aalborg University (AAU, Denmark) where he is an associate professor and leads the MeCIS (Media Cognition and Interactive Systems) research group. He is founder and director of the Augmented Cognition Laboratory, dedicated to the study of perception, cognition, and affective states in relation to immersive media and cognitive and "extended realities" (XR) technologies. Currently he participates in various European projects with a line of research dedicated to the study of narrative cognition in digital culture using neuroscientific methods. Between 2011 and 2017 he was elected president of the Nordic Association for Semiotic Studies for three consecutive terms, being a recognized expert in cognitive and cultural semiotics with experience in interactive narratives, communication sciences and cognitive sciences.

From 2004 to 2016 he was an external collaborating professor at the Institute of Molecular Biology of the University of Copenhagen, developing and teaching science theory modules to numerous classes of biologists.

Preface to the English edition of liquid risks

Liquid Risks was first published in Spanish in 2022, just two years ago, and in such a short time, so much has happened in the world that editing it in an English version was more an exercise of updating and even revising than translating. Even though the core ideas and most of the texts are the same as in the Spanish version, the acceleration of the artificial intelligence applications and the new landscape of conflicts on the planet somehow demonstrate what I expressed in the book proves itself correct: Liquid risks are hardly predictable and containable.

This book is about a category of risks that have emerged unnoticed out of the uncertainty and complexity that have spread out filling the most remote places of our accelerated world. I define them as liquid precisely because they are hard to contain but, at the same time, are highly adaptable to change, which means a significant challenge to people, organizations, and nations.

I have dedicated most of my life to think and act in terms of security. In my career, I have seen how risks have evolved from predictable causes and straightforward analysis to anonymous threats and undetectable vulnerabilities. As intangible as these risks might be, their consequences are real, with costs that transcend conventional estimations.

Traditional methods of risk identification, rooted in passive observation and delayed response, prove ineffective in this evolving environment. The advent of globalization, the rise of transnational terrorist groups, and the pervasive cyber threats have led entire nations to recognize the obsolescence of segmented and isolated intelligence models.

History imparts valuable lessons about the dangers of solely concentrating on visible threats. During the Cold War, intelligence efforts were focused on gauging the adversary's offensive capabilities without considering the system's overall health. The most emblematic example is the 1989 collapse of the Berlin Wall. Despite the Soviet Union's outwardly robust military strength, its economy and societal fabric had become unsustainable. Intelligence analysts failed to foresee this event, underscoring the need for a more comprehensive perspective.

Under the liquid scope, the 9/11 attacks, Cambridge Analytica, and mass migrations fit in the morphology of this new kind of danger; they sprung from multiple forces acting together, accelerated by globalization and hyperconnectivity, and cloaked by apparent chaos, making them unharness under linear risk assessment models.

Through the book's pages, you will read concepts you are probably unfamiliar with. Some of them are: acceleration, uncertainty gap, securization, heterarchy, and multiplexation. I had to develop this new vocabulary to build a framework under which we can begin to understand not only the very nature of liquid risks but also the surrounding context they come from. Within the framework of fluidity, we must go beyond understanding to fully grasp the liquid risks. Even though recognizing them and developing awareness is fundamental, new mindsets, leadership, structures and visions are paramount to survive and succeed in this challenge. From individuals to governments, anticipation and a transformative approach to reality are just a few of the immense adaptation processes that must be made.

The reader will find many examples throughout the chapters to better illustrate the liquid risks. Some belong to my personal experience in Venezuela, my homeland—a country I cannot return to while the Chavista regime remains in power. I discovered firsthand that liquid risks are mainly linked to those who tyrannically rule organizations or nations. Once the concept that shapes liquidity is understood, new examples will emerge in every reader's mind.

Two new chapters were added to the English version of Liquid Risks: From the Matrix to Liquid Wars and Living with an Artificial Alien. Both expand the realms of these risks into new frontiers. Wars are the favorite territory of those looking to strengthen power, and meanwhile, AI is still in the process of becoming a new kind of entity; the energy unleashed is so enormous that it can throw humanity to an unforeseen stage of development or on the verge of its destruction.

Risks are always a probability, and today, more than ever, the possibility of having a better world depends entirely on us. Humanity is not predetermined to catastrophic destiny, but the magnitude of the risks has, long ago, trespassed our capability to mitigate them; now, it is urgent to harness them and learn to live with them as if they would be a Damocles sword hanging over our heads.

Tampa, Florida
April 2024

Introduction

It was in January 2017, during a lecture on future risks and security given by a retired general of the United States Army in Washington, DC, when I first heard about intangible risks. The general referred to a class of dangers invisible to the ordinary people, that were bred under some of the premises of sustainable development and could spread without control. In his presentation, he denoted the growing negative impact that the interconnected processes of accelerated globalization and technological explosion had on people and organizations. Even though there were more and more signs that something was going on, we did not realize what we had ahead. And what was even worse, amid our ignorance, we enjoyed walking the tightrope of these new and strange threats while we lived unaware of the effects generated by such risks. Of course, among the examples that the general presented to the audience were new forms of terrorism, the use of the Dark Web as a platform for illegal arms trafficking, human trafficking networks operated from applications on mobile phones, and the manipulation of news specifically designed to change the opinion of certain social groups. But of all the issues covered in that conference, what caught my attention the most was the phrase written on the last slide of his presentation: We have entered a world for which they have made us believe that we are prepared, and about which we ignore almost everything, where the major strength of these threats, even anonymous, is to keep us deceived in the cloak of our arrogance. I was not only impressed but also concerned by what I had heard, even more so when the words came from an officer who, until recently, had been an active member of the most powerful military machine in the world.

Those ideas of intangible risks easily stuck in my mind, although I didn't know how to interpret them or what to do with them for a while. Then, at the beginning of 2020, came the WHO declaration of the COVID-19 pandemic. Those were days when the entire world slowed down, almost to a stop, in the midst of unprecedented levels of planetary uncertainty. It was then that phrases such as anonymous threats or the ignorance of our arrogance began to make sense in my thoughts. For the next six months, I was locked up, like most people everywhere else on Earth, in a tiny place. I was living in an apartment close to Tampa International Airport in Florida. For weeks, I did not hear an airplane. At night, I would go out to the two-square-meter balcony that overlooked a sort of internal patio of the building that I shared with about twenty neighbors, most of them younger than me and who, simultaneously, in a ritual of collective relaxation, would smoke leisurely a joint of weed, in what seemed to me their particular search for answers on an obscure reality. In that somewhat thick context, I began to share with my neighbors the idea that we were surrounded by intangible dangers and risks that no longer belonged to a distant future but that we were rather experiencing in real time.

Today, four years after those sessions, I do not know if my fellow members understood me or if they even paid attention at all. In any case, that was a beneficial experience because, by putting so many disordered ideas into words, these began to take shape in a structure that I had already defined as liquid risks. With this extended essay on risks, initially written in short articles and now compiled in a book, I try to address the consequences of the accelerated change in the world in recent years from my own experience based on three decades as a security consultant. A world marked by anonymous threats, uncertainty, and complexity, in which we came to believe, before the pandemic, that we had managed to hold reality under control when the truth was that we covered ourselves with the cloak of our arrogance.

In the analysis, I have tried to maintain a broad and realistic vision of the complex dynamics that move our world. Through explanations, definitions, and examples, I attempt to outline some ideas to classify these risks, to make the dangers underlying the globalization process more visible, and to create awareness about their existence and, from there, build some strategies to address them, analyze them, and, if possible, mitigate them. These are methods that, in new times, we could call liquid security tools aimed at translating complexity into signals we can read to make more timely and accurate decisions. In two years of reflection and research on the topic, I have seen how the pandemic has further accelerated the advance of complexity, and the virus is an example of the materialization of liquid, intangible, and uncontainable risks with devastating effects.

But I have been interested in exploring another, even more liquid aspect of this phenomenon. It is about how threats linked to power use the phenomena of complexity to become more robust and more adaptive. I have discovered that the new risks of the liquid world need the substrate of complex systems to survive and expand, hence the importance of understanding the properties of a reality that is no longer linear and from which change emerges in an unstoppable and unpredictable way. Among the risks of complexity tied to power, we find the new liquid totalitarian projects. These are, until recently, unknown expressions of organization in which multiple interests converge, which, without any scruple, tyrannize countries and regions in ways that democratic States have not been able to contain, much less defeat.

The spread of risks in this era of complexity does not only occur in countries and large organizations. It has an extraordinary impact on individuals, who are the first victims as they become out of step with the accelerated pace of change imposed by globalization. This is how, in a world in permanent transit, where everything is defined in terms of flows and connections, human beings suffer the great paradox of living entangled in dozens of social networks while isolating themselves in a profound individualism, now stimulated by remote work, the distancing and reduction of direct interpersonal relationships due to the regulations aimed at containing the pandemic, and the autocratic use that many governments decided to make of them.

I have tried to make this essay easy to read without too many technicalities or academicisms. However, I must confess that it has been a significant effort of synthesis since the topic has a variety of dimensions and can be approached from multiple angles. In my case, I chose to stay in my professional field, which is security. With humility, I have barely touched on topics of sociology, philosophy, and physics, which are not my areas of expertise but ones that I am passionate about, and this has triggered in me a yearning to investigate and learn more.

The book is assembled into 19 chapters, some of which I published previously as short articles and essays on my blog, albertoray.com.

4

Although they are independent of each other, together they build a narrative that aims to explain the liquid world and its risks.

Finally, I have assumed a priori that liquid risks are in the present time and will shortly be the most critical challenge global security will face. Therefore, the sooner we understand and get a deep awareness of their impacts, the more successful we can be in our attempt to contain and mitigate them. However, if there is one thing we must keep in mind, it is that, as the general said in 2017, the greatest strength of these liquid threats is to make us believe that we are prepared when we have been cloaked in ignorance and the mantle of arrogance.

I hope that my colleagues, whom I call the risk professionals, as well as those belonging to other closer professions and interested individuals, will gain in these pages the necessary motivation to keep their eyes firmly on the horizon, as the old lookouts did at the top of the masts of ancient ships, scanning for potential dangers and charting the route to safe harbors. I also hope that all those friends of mine who are not risk professionals will enjoy this book.

Alberto Ray

Tampa, April 2022

1

Danger! There are no borders

No man ever steps into the same river twice,
for it's not the river and
he's not the same man.

-Heraclitus

We could assume that everything linked to human action and its interactions is the subject of sociology. Even climate change or the appearance of new diseases, which until a few decades ago were not associated with social tasks, are now considered sociological phenomena because man is no longer seen as alien to nature but has become an active agent in the modification of the environment or the spread of pandemics enhanced by the effects of globalization. The fact is that global warming and infectious diseases existed even before humans populated the Earth. What makes the analysis different now is the probability that we are the ones who can, in some way, do something to stop, mitigate or soften its effects. And thus provide humanity with a safer future. However, if we do not act according to what science and technology dictates, we could also worsen the situation and precipitate a catastrophe. There is also the possibility that the human species and its actions in the present can modify the future and make it better or worse, depending on the degree of awareness we have today (of the short, mid, or long-term consequences of our actions). In this sense, we have become agents of risk, not only limited to potential events that can change the course of life on Earth, but we have assumed the immense responsibility that the decisions of the present will determine the welfare of future generations. And, no matter how insignificant these decisions may seem, they will place a weight on our shoulders that will define us as a society.

Ulrich Beck (1944 - 2015), a German sociologist who developed his career at the London School of Economics, was the first to propose risk as a category that defined society. In his book Risk Society, Beck argues that our society is no longer defined in socioeconomic or cultural terms. Instead, he argues, societies live according to the opportunities or threats derived from strategies for addressing risks. According to Beck, in industrialized societies, conflicts are no longer linked to the distribution of wealth but rather to the distribution of risks. Individuals have left behind the risks related to poverty and have entered a class of ecological risks caused by the control of nature through technological development.

Beck points out that humans have reached a stage in development where we have created risks we cannot contain. His thesis came at the right time because it was in 1986 that the explosion of the Chernobyl nuclear power plant in Ukraine took place, and this gave strength to his vision of society's responsibility for its future. Beck's approaches were refuted by several thinkers since, for many, it was not new that societies experienced or created risks that they could not control or dominate. Among his critics was Niklas Luhmann, a German sociologist (1927–1998) who developed a systemic theory of society emphasizing the idea that social facts could not necessarily be considered actions of society since only individuals could perform actions. Therefore, the unit of observation of sociology should not be facts. For Luhmann, communication is the only genuinely social phenomenon (because it is shared with more than one individual). According to Luhmann, risk arises from uncertainty or a lack of trust between two or more individuals. Thus, the only way to mitigate such risks would be for the individuals to share the same set of values and norms, and that would only be possible through socialization, that is, communication. Luhmann defines risk through a binary concept. He establishes that what is not risky is not necessarily safe since there could be non-risky phenomena that are nevertheless not safe. Thus, Luhmann ends up arriving at the risk/danger binomial. Luhmann establishes that **risk is the likely damage that arises as a consequence of a decision, while danger is something external that depends on the environment**. Therefore, whereas for Beck, risk is a characteristic associated with the nature of society, for Luhmann, whose approach is Systems Theory, risk is a characteristic that is shaped by each society's cultural approach to decision making. Ulrich Beck, in subsequent analyses to Risk Society, and responding to criticism, developed a broader theory, which he called Reflexive Modernity, or Second Modernity. Beck expected it to be seen as an evolution (not a revolution, as Marx proposed) of industrial modernity and is based on three structural premises:

- In industrial modernity, societies are divided into national States that are their territorial and institutional "containers."

- In general, industrial modernity gives value to the collective and social stratification, and although the concept of the individual appears, it is still very limited.

- Industrial modernity is constituted in commercial-capitalist societies where paid work and full employment become the highest aspiration.

That first modernity was built on the assumption that nature was external to society and could be exploited without limit. Beck considers that science is focused on the domination of nature and that scientists monopolize knowledge. From there, a hierarchy is established that separates experts from laymen. As a last assumption, modern society faces the complexity of the world by establishing a functional division between the areas of knowledge, which is why it marks an obvious difference between economics, science, politics, etc. In contrast to the first modernity, the premises of reflexive modernity emerge to generate a new framework for society. According to Beck, this new modernity creates a reflexive society based on three theorems: risk society, forced individualization, and multidimensional globalization. Within this context, my main interest is risk society research because it is the foundation for developing my vision of liquid risks. However, both the phenomena of individualization and globalization are essential to understanding the liquid world, based on Zygmunt Bauman's metaphor, extensively discussed in his works on Liquid Modernity.

Bauman was a Polish sociologist (1925–2017) who, in his long career, made a lucid analysis of postmodernity or liquid modernity, a term he coined to define the profound changes in the direction that society has taken, its ways of life and the way of perceiving the world. For Bauman, "we have left behind an ancient or solid modernity, of immutable truths and predictable times, to fall seduced by impermanence, mutation, simulacrum, the absence of truth and the end of the structuring stories." The consequence of the liquid is the erosion of the bonds between human beings, which has made the ideas of community and identity obsolete. The metaphor of liquid explains the new dynamics of society. Today's society is marked by relationships that are in permanent transit: liquid love, liquid art, liquid culture, and liquid surveillance. About individualism, Bauman is almost nostalgic for a (traditional) modernity that will no longer return. He considers the loss of ties between individuals a weakness. In a liquid world characterized by rapid and unpredictable flow, we need, more than ever, firm and reliable bonds of friendship and mutual trust.

The expansion of borders after globalization hides a gray area of ambivalence, turning the planet, according to Bauman, into an archipelago of diasporas. They are new migrations with a big question about the link between identity and citizenship, between the individual and the territory. Technology, for its part, contributes to this system of mutual exclusions of societies that, while they connect on social networks, unravel in their relationships. Under this rapid overview, risk can no longer be considered a phenomenon extrinsic to society but has become the price that must be paid to evolve from a traditional modernity to a more advanced one. Risk is the necessary commitment (trade-off) that forces one to give up a position to achieve another that is assumed to be more advantageous. We have thus transformed ourselves into a risk society because, in some way, risk is inherent to the social dynamics of these times. Whether from doing or communicating, the common currency values some individuals over others. Whoever takes the most risks places themselves in the zone of greatest uncertainty but also of greatest profit, which is why risk ends up being so addictive. Although Bauman never explicitly referred to liquid risks, his vision of impermanent society, immersed in a mutant space where nothing is everlasting, frames—with open edges—the dimension in which liquid risks unfold.

In the present research, it has become evident that behind the hyperconnectivity of society and technological development, intangible dangers with unimaginable consequences and transformative effects for countries, their populations, and even their geographies have been brewing and hiding. To facilitate understanding, I chose the term **liquid risks**, taking as a point of reference Bauman's metaphor which, with his description of the Liquid World, sets the context in which these risks, many of them intangible, are created, are deployed, and materialize their powerful effects.

11

Early in my research I realized that liquid risks had their genesis in the gap that had opened between the acceleration of the complexity of the hyperconnected and technologically advanced world–understood by a few–and the majority who are displaced from a world they do not understand. Terrorism is not the only global phenomenon that exploits the advantages of this liquid world. Liquid risks also materialize in the polarization of international and domestic politics, the leadership forged by social networks, the development of tools linked to big data and artificial intelligence, and the dissemination of alternative truths from influential media outlets, to mention just a few. All of this builds up a reality that is not static anymore but that rather behaves as a fluid that passes through us without stopping to wait for us, in an apparent charm that we cannot resist but contains the greatest danger. We have become agents of pervasive risks over which we have no control.

...these new threats can appear in the liquid world and, as soon as we perceive them, instantly fade, leaving us, in some cases, with the idea that they were just the outcome of a delusion.

2

A trip in the car of complexity

*If everything seems to be under control,
You're not going fast enough*

-Mario Andretti

In 1967, the renowned American author Roger Zelazny published a science fiction novel called Lord of Light. The novel's plot revolves around a group of revolutionaries who plan to take society to a higher level of development using advanced technologies. Zelazny called them accelerationists. They believe that humanity can achieve great things, but its limitations are currently holding it back. They also believe that by using advanced technologies, humanity can overcome these limitations and achieve its full potential. The accelerationists are a controversial group, with some believing their ideas are dangerous and others thinking they are the key to humanity's future.

"...Accelerationism — it is a simple doctrine of sharing. It proposes that we of Heaven give unto those who dwell below our knowledge and powers and substance. This act of charity would be directed to raising their condition of existence to a higher level, akin to that which we occupy. Then every man would be a god, you see. The result of this, of course, would be that there would no longer be any gods, only men."

At this point in the 21st century, few people remember Zelazny, but, as novelist J.G.Ballard once wrote, what science fiction authors invent today, you and I will do tomorrow. Surprisingly, accelerationism later became a major movement that preached the need to evolve toward a post-capitalist world marked by the continued dynamics of change. More than 50 years later, impressively confirming Ballard's quote, what was fiction in the sixties of the 20th century is now part of our most everyday reality. The technological version of accelerationism is a trend of thought that asserts that accelerating the development and adoption of advanced technologies is beneficial for overcoming social and economic problems. Andy Beckett, a British journalist, builds a stylized profile of accelerationists:

Accelerationists argue that technology, particularly computer technology, and capitalism, particularly the most aggressive, global variety, should be massively sped up and intensified – either because this is the best way forward for humanity or because there is no alternative. Accelerationists favor automation. They favor the further merging of the digital and the human. They often favor the deregulation of business and drastically scaled-back government. They believe that people should stop deluding themselves that economic and technological progress can be controlled. They often believe that social and political upheaval has a value in itself.

However, there is no uniform criterion regarding its consequences. Some advocates argue that accelerating automation and artificial intelligence will liberate humanity from monotonous and repetitive tasks, allowing for greater allocation of resources to more creative and meaningful activities. Others, on the contrary, warn about the potential ethical risks associated with rapid technological advancement and its effects on exacerbating the gap between those who control the process and those held by the hyper-technologization of society.

Today, no one can remain indifferent to change. Either because of the interest it arouses or the resistance it gives rise to, we cannot disregard it due to both its capacity to alter the environment as well as the profound impact it has on the life course of those living on the planet, and contemporary society has assumed change as a constant. With or without awareness, everything changes at a greater pace. The change, furthermore, is invigorated by the acceleration with which it occurs and is the central axis of a new global dynamic that makes everything more complex. Acceleration and complexity are intrinsic to change, and both operate in a synergy that enhances them. Still, it is worth asking how this acceleration and complexity of change are manifested. How do they impact people and organizations? Accelerated change may seem most palpable in technology. It is enough to observe the expansion of telecommunications, the availability, and accessibility of information, or the growing processing and storage capacities of electronic microcomponents to intuit this ubiquity of change. However, change is also present in the new ways of doing business, the different ways societies organize and participate in public life, and even the types of government countries have. All these forces, with the power to transform the life of every man and woman on Earth, are interdependent and feed off each other in their complexities, producing an infinite network of possibilities and non-linear relationships between causes and effects, making the surrounding reality increasingly less intelligible.

It is worth highlighting that the accelerated growth in the number of members participating in a system and the increased interactions between these members are conditions for complexity. However, the difficulty in describing the behavior of the elements (members) that constitute it further increases the system's complexity. Even if we know the details of a situation and its actors, if this reality is complex, we cannot predict the future behavior of any reality (system) with a reasonable degree of precision. The increasing pace at which changes occur is accompanied—because it is one of its consequences—by the dissolution of what is permanent. As Zygmunt Bauman points out:

> *Modern society cannot maintain its shape or direction for a long time; everything in it is ephemeral, and its members change before the ways of acting are consolidated into certain habits and routines.*

Then, a sort of addiction to change appeared, dividing the world into two classes of individuals separated by an abysmal void. On the one hand, some move around the globe as smoothly as if they were moving between the backyard and the front door of their own house; they are the global nomads. They inhabit the global realm, they think globally, and they have been able to develop a synoptic vision (understanding) of reality, mostly a virtualized vision of reality without spatial or temporal limits. On the other hand, there are the locals. They are those who remain anchored to the territory they occupy as well as to the physical time. Neither the globals can nor interested in acting locally, nor are the locals interested nor capable of thinking globally. Different sets of skills are needed to engage with each realm fruitfully. Therefore, we live in a reality that no longer configures a solid and invariable state but in one that has been transformed (as we perceive it) into a fluid in transit in which nothing remains on the stage for too long as if everything were under the action of a continuous mutation that devalues what comes before and makes unpredictable what happens next. Thus, the gap between those who lead the change and those who ignore its consequences is part of that liquid world that has lost its handles and references. Within this gap, a category of risks that we will call liquid risks was born. To date, we have not yet found effective formulas to mitigate them, given the difficulty in understanding, defining, and addressing them. Still, the present book aims to provide its readers with an understanding of their nature, approaches to classify them, and preliminary tools to deal with them, although on a case-by-case basis. The challenge facing those who are called to manage this new risk category is formidable. Not only because of the intangibility of the threats and the liquid dynamics in which they operate but also because of their capacities to adapt to the environment.

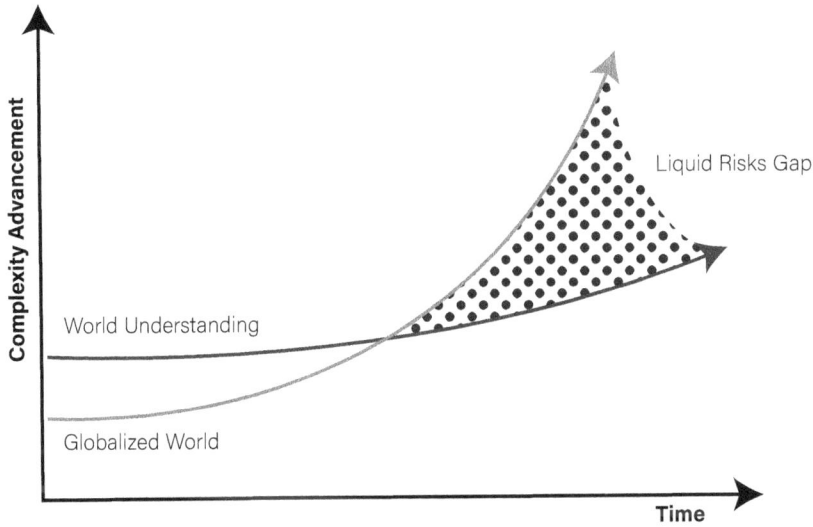

Figure 1: The liquid risk formation gap

We were used to dealing with solid and tangible threats. In a reality where changes had a face and were differentiated from their environment, they functioned in a defined temporal and spatial framework, and concerning their modes of operation, it was even possible to predict some of their movements. In contrast, these new threats can appear in the liquid world and, as soon as we perceive them, instantly fade, leaving us, in some cases, with the idea that they were just the outcome of a delusion. They blend in with their environment and cross-temporal and spatial boundaries through the globalized networks that interconnect everything. Its incomprehension derives from the complexity of the liquid world.

Both complexity and incomprehension feed off each other in an accelerated dynamic that places the individual amid the greatest uncertainty, and from there, the individual becomes a vulnerable subject for those who decide to exploit his lack of ability to understand (and predict) the immediate future. This is how liquid risks are built and strengthened in a recursive cycle, and uncertainty works as the axis, leading us to lose all reference to the predictable environment.

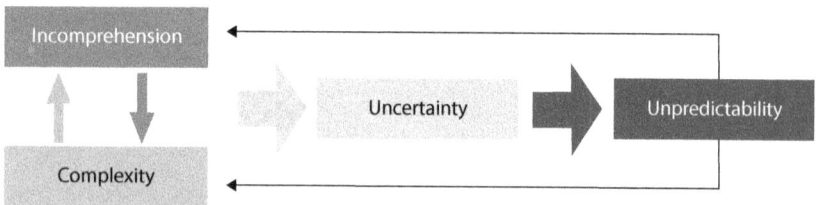

Figure 2: Formation cycle of liquid risks

Global terrorism, revealed in the events of September 11, 2001, was perhaps the first liquid threat of the millennium. From there, multiple phenomena have surprised humanity with very high costs in lives, material goods, and loss of trust, reputation, and institutions. We could predict that all risks will be liquid in the future, even though many of them already impact us in the present. The complexity of globalization includes the accelerated technological development of artificial intelligence, advances in genetic manipulation, and the explosion of social networks. However, there are also more undefined risks that are difficult to calibrate. These include the effects of post-truths, presented as facts but not supported by evidence; populist leaderships that grow like foam; and hybrid wars, portrayed as conflicts fought using conventional and unconventional methods, such as propaganda, cyberwarfare, lawfare, and economic sanctions, as well as the destruction of reputations in a matter of hours through viral messages that can be used to spread misinformation, promote hate speech, or damage the reputation of individuals or organizations.

A significant part of this process occurs in the dimension of the immaterial and in front of our eyes, without us being truly capable of seeing it. It is the substitution of the world of atoms by the world of bits encoded as information and knowledge, which is the maximum expression of power for liquid society.

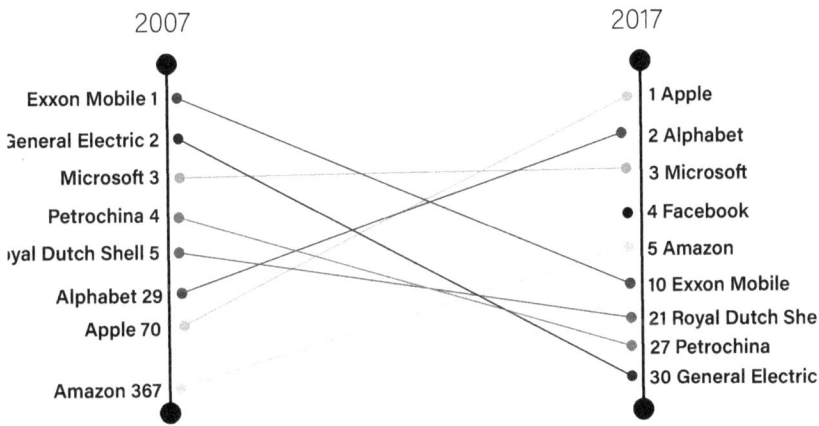

2007	2017
Exxon Mobile 1	1 Apple
General Electric 2	2 Alphabet
Microsoft 3	3 Microsoft
Petrochina 4	4 Facebook
Royal Dutch Shell 5	5 Amazon
Alphabet 29	10 Exxon Mobile
Apple 70	21 Royal Dutch She
Amazon 367	27 Petrochina
	30 General Electric

Figure 3: The transition from the economy of atoms to the economy of bits (2007-2017)

RAND Corporation, the policy think tank favored by the US Department of Defense, coined the term Truth Decay to describe truth's diminished role in American public life today. "The breakdown of truth has joined the new lexicon that includes phrases like fake news or alternative truths." Today, we are on the threshold of a reality we are only beginning to know. We need to understand it before fully addressing new methods to mitigate these risks. Hence, it is essential to create awareness of the nature of the actors that

21

drive these new threats. These are the challenges liquid scenarios have brought, in which nothing lasts long, and the acceleration of change erases everything that seeks to establish itself as permanent.

Some skeptics of accelerationism believe that the rate and mode of change in the present time are not dramatically different from those in the past, so the impact of the pace of change on the lives of individuals and societies living in the present is overestimated. The fact that the world has gone through accelerated times and will likely go through other waves of accelerated times in the future is indisputable. The current case is not unique, but it has particular characteristics that render it quite different from previous ones. The most significant thing is that now, acceleration occurs in a globalized world, with unprecedented development and technological convergence, with immediate availability of unlimited information, and amid an explosion of connectivity enhanced by social networks. No matter how distant they may be, people located anywhere in the world are today dramatically more reachable than in the past. However, this accelerated pace of change did not arrive by chance. It has been cooked slowly, and at some moment in the recent past, it went through a turning point that energized it. American author Thomas Friedman argues that in June 2007, with the launch of the iPhone, humanity's first smartphone, history accelerated.

"...there are special years for wines, and there are special years for history, and 2007 was one of them. Not only due to the emergence of the iPhone, a large group of companies emerged around that year. Companies and their innovations have reconfigured how people and machines communicate, create, collaborate, and think".

It is possible that this was the case, that in 2007, the rate of changes increased. A convergence took place, in time and space, of an immense flow of energy that was transformed into high-tech industry advances, such as the manufacture of electronic microcomponents with integrated circuitry on a single chip, the innovation in programming languages, the emergence of new operating systems in computer science and the expansion of digital telecommunications networks. The convergence launched humanity into an accelerated dynamic.

The metaphor of a boiling pot can help explain that the processes of change in societies, and even more so when the rate of change is accelerated, do not occur out of nowhere. Instead, they originate in a set of forces previously accumulating in the social and economic fabric. Just as the pot of water does not boil until the heat has been applied for a while, so too societies do not change until the forces of change have been building up for some time. These forces can be economic, political, social, or technological. When they reach a certain point, a sort of transformative stage, they can cause a sudden and dramatic change, quite often not easy to predict. This is why it is important to be aware of the forces of change that are at work in our society (in the present) so that we can be prepared for the changes that may come (in the future). An example of what is stated here is the fall of the Berlin Wall. For more than three decades in the European countries under Soviet rule, multiple forces of social change had been manifesting that, when repressed or frustrated, as happened in Hungary in 1956 or in the Prague Spring in 1968, could not be transformed, but rather they silently piled up and matured until their sudden explosion in 1989, breaking down not only the physical barriers that divided these countries from their environment but also liberating the countries from communism.

The year 2007 can be seen as the culmination of technological development, specifically telecommunications and globalization. The iPhone embodied these forces, and it accelerated the pace of change. In the past, when change was slower, we felt we had more control over our environment; we understood it better and could predict the future more accurately. However, with the arrival of this

23

newly accelerated pace of change, predicting the future became more complex. We are now constantly bombarded with new information and technologies, and it can be hard to keep up. This ignorance can be a source of anxiety for some people, but it also means that there are endless possibilities for the future. Gone are the linear times in which there was proportionality between causes and effects. Likewise, there have been other times when the pace of change has been so slow that it has seemed like reality was always the same and operated as if it were independent of time. Those were the periods in history when time froze. Jean Piaget, a Swiss biologist and child psychologist, explained that the notion of time in the child arises from the experience of movement:

"This is born as different or identical spatial positions, successive or simultaneous...we can, therefore, establish a parallelism between time and place. The notions of before, after, and now are linked to those of in front, behind, or here. "

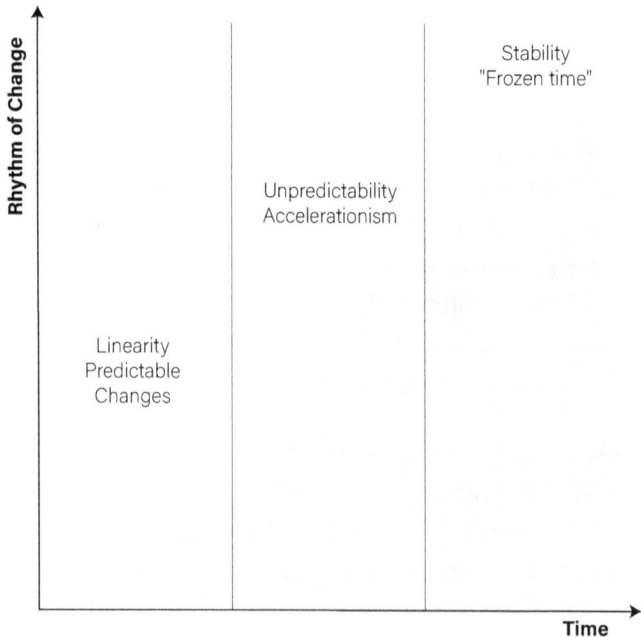

Figure 4
The pace of change: Linearity - Unpredictability - Stability

In line with Piaget's concepts, we could argue that what we perceive as an acceleration of time is rather a product of the accelerated movement of the liquid world. The contraction of space on the planet, caused by globalization and fed back by technological development, changed the perception of time, and the signs indicate that this change is in its beginnings and has a lot of accumulated energy, which predicts a long journey. A fascinating angle of this dynamic in the changing pace of time is that accelerated periods of unpredictability do not necessarily occur after linear processes of change. It could actually happen that a stable one follows a linear period without going through an accelerated interval. This acceleration can be unpredictable and could lead to major transformation processes in civilizations, such as revolutions, natural catastrophes, or great wars. In addition to the notion of the change in the rhythm of time, it is worth highlighting a rather curious phenomenon known as takinesis. Those who suffer from it perceive episodes of accelerated reality around them. This can be a very disturbing experience, making the person feel like they are losing control of their reality. Takinetic individuals will describe it as if the movements occurred more quickly than usual. Referring to the accelerated perception of time is, in a way, a metaphor since there is no sense of time, like smell, sight, or touch, to prove it, and it probably happens through the circadian rhythms of the organism, such as the brain. It keeps track of the lapses between one event and another. Takinesia is linked to physiological and neurological causes associated with increased body temperature and some types of migraine. However, there is a type of takinesis related to the extrinsic activation of the sense of time, and although research on the subject is scarce, reality points to simultaneity and multitasking facilitated through technological platforms and the ability to mutate between things. Real and virtual are some of the causes of accelerationism in current times.

I had my first direct experience of liquid risks in 2014. At that time, I was working as a security advisor in an office building located in downtown Caracas. For ten years, I accompanied a client in a progressive process of improvements in the protection of the building, which at the time housed about 175 private companies and a few public organizations. During that time, we minimized security incidents by incorporating technology and training security personnel. Likewise, we significantly raised the preventive culture of users. Among our most valuable assets, we had a very well-designed and maintained automated access control. It allowed us to record more than ten thousand transactions daily, becoming our system's backbone. During a weekend, when we had scheduled a system maintenance window and a brief connection through the Internet for updating, an alert message appeared on the server screen: YOUR DATA HAS BEEN HELD HOSTAGE – PAY 15 BITCOINS TO RELEASE. It was my first experience with a ransomware case. Even though we were able to restore the database without paying the ransom and with a minimal loss of information, that day, we understood that we were naked in the face of new and powerful threats and that we had to address those new threats soon; otherwise, we would not only instantly lose our information, but also the security model that had taken us a decade to build it. The tip of a gigantic iceberg was beginning to emerge.

The main obstacle to defining a secure future is disconnecting the static analysis of reality from the dynamic and mutating nature of the threats. We cannot approach the future thinking that tomorrow will be identical to today.

3

Classification of liquid risks

Building taxonomies is always a challenge. Often, we may incur the risk of classifying the diversity of things in the World as the mythic Chinese emperor did. That emperor, according to Jorge Luis Borges, classified animals into: "(a) those that belong to the Emperor, (b) embalmed ones, (c) those that are trained, (d) suckling pigs, (e) mermaids, (f) fabulous ones, (g) stray dogs, (h) those that are included in the present classification, (i) those that tremble as if they are mad, (j) innumerable ones, (k) those drawn with a very thin camel hair brush, (l) others, (m) those that have just broken a flower vase, (n) those that look like flies from a long way off". This caveat is to warn readers that what I am presenting here is just an early attempt to classify something that is fuzzy, vague, and elusive.

Having said that, I will start by noting that liquid risks can be grouped differently, given their mutant nature. Therefore, it is difficult to contain them within very specific parameters and categories. The proposed classification is based on five categories: Technological, economic, political, social, and criminal. Since most of these risks are mixed (meaning that they are not pure categories), the best way to represent them is by overlapping each other. The overlaps may not only be double, but they can be triple (this is the case of some kinds of fake news systematically disseminated through digital media to influence the behavior of the population) and even quadruple or quintuple (as in some forms of terrorism or the exercise of sophisticated tools of social control in totalitarian regimes). In fact, it is possible that many of the new risks will be liquid. Likewise, there are already known risks that have never been labeled, but they are liquid and have been present in our societies for a long time. The experience with the ransomware I described in the previous chapter was a liquid risk associated with a new technology that had an economic and criminal impact. Below, I list some examples of liquid risks generated by human action:

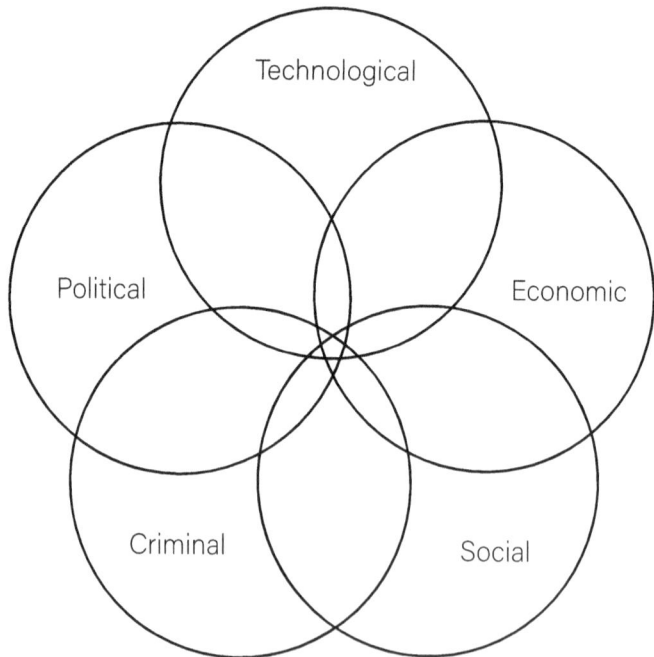

Figure 5: Overlapping of liquid risks

Political

We are in the presence of political risks when we realize that politics has become malleable and that political actors may take advantage of the complexity and uncertainty of the environment and use it to advance their particular agendas. These risks are expressed in the transformation of politics as a spectacle and are made intangible through instruments such as disinformation; however, they have very tangible effects such as intimidation, repression or control of society. Examples of these risks are: intimidating social control, new forms of populism, the transformations of republics into criminal States, the denaturation of regular armies, the manipulation of electoral systems, a diversity of new methods for legitimizing dictatorships, the creation of narratives aimed at changing history; the polarization and construction of internal enemies.

Economic

The economy is one of the most complex spaces in the liquid and globalized world. Hence, there is relative ease in forming risks linked to the flow of capital from illicit activities or the use of new digital platforms for converting currencies into cryptocurrencies under the protection of anonymity. At their origin, these risks usually arise from the actions of agents who, pursuing their own interests, exploit the political and technological advantages of the globalized world through the manipulation of markets, technological platforms, and narratives. Some examples of these risks are: New market platforms for crime (Dark Web), the use of cryptocurrencies as means of payment, the globalization of crime and its institutions amongst many others.

Social

This category of liquid risks is usually associated with the instrumentalization and exploitation of society, especially of those who are most vulnerable to ideological or political action. These risks can also arise from the polarization of human groups

31

fostered by information technology and, particularly, digital social networks. Social liquid risks also have an impact on the blurring of the line separating the public from the private. Examples of these risks are: Human trafficking, in some cases used as destabilizing tools aimed at undermining social, economic, and political systems of nations and regions; new forms of consumerism; cancel culture; destruction of reputations through social networks; new forms of slavery; liquefaction of laws and regulations; securitization of society (aimed at instilling fear by making people believe that investments in security are never enough compared to the level of the threats); gradual blurring of the border between the public and the private spheres, criminal pax, the creation of narratives aimed at modifying history.

Technological

Technological acceleration is one of the threats from which liquid risks are generated. The gap between those who control the technology and those who use it is slowly growing. From it, unimaginable amounts of information are manipulated for the benefit of the former, giving them an advantage. Examples of liquid risks linked to technology are biometric surveillance, uncontrolled and ethically unrestricted quantum computing developments, genetic engineering, and artificial intelligence (more on these risks below, in chapter on AI and liquid risks).

Criminal

Usually these risks arise from threats that exploit the advantages of the complex and accelerated world. These threats are characterized by anonymity, having extensive capabilities to operate globally, and organizing themselves in diffuse networks. Examples of these risks are: New forms of terrorism, globalization of crime, expansion of gray zones and dissolution of territorial borders, the proliferation of designer drugs and growth of the markets, and narratives aimed at legalizing criminal activities.

Since liquid risks are difficult to identify, it is not easy to make a catalog of them. The categories and examples of liquid risks listed above approximate patterns and cases currently relevant to the public. Some of them, as controversial as genetic manipulation in human beings, are especially sensitive to public opinion. Others, no less important, have been absolutely unnoticed, stealthy growing and spreading out across countries and continents. Examples of these risks are: New forms of slavery and global networks of pedophilia through the Internet. The first approach to developing the necessary awareness of liquid risks is identifying them. This book aims to be part of the initial definition process of these risks.

Liquid risks, mingled

Liquid risks are essentially global and not easy to separate one from the other. They are omnipresent, although they are not obvious to the eye. In this book we examine those most closely linked to the political realms, focusing on a case that directly impacts every individual's life, liberty, and well-being. However, as we have already mentioned, given the degree of entanglement of the risk with its environment, the analysis demands a more complete vision of its consequences. Consider, for example, intimidating social control. It refers to the power that governments exercise to limit freedoms, using a wide range of laws, repressive actions, social programs, and even sophisticated information technologies aimed mainly at controlling the behavior of citizens. It is a carefully designed conditioning system with a mixture of punishments and rewards, with the objective of extinguishing inconvenient or uncomfortable behaviors for the rulers.

Although social control is an ancient technique, the conditioning of citizens through the use of technological platforms for mobile phones, which are mandatory to access basic citizen services, have the ultimate purpose of capturing personal data. Eventually, this data may be used to profile and predict the sympathy (or the animosity) of citizens towards the government. Depending on this information, the individual is initially encouraged or intimidated to moderate her behavior, allowing or limiting her access to public transportation systems, social benefits, jobs, health services, etc. All of this is interconnected, in one way or another, to the same big data platform where AI algorithms are deployed.

Something much more sophisticated is practiced by the Chinese Communist Party using a points system that adds or subtracts from the inhabitants, and depending on results, people will have access to privileges that are granted, such as buying pets and choosing their children's schools or taking vacations in certain places. As can be seen, framing liquid risks is not so simple because they mutate, adapt and transform according to the environments where they are deployed, and their effects are uncontainable by those who decide to exploit them.

A unique example of liquid risk fusion occurred between November 2020 and January 2021, when the world experienced the events of the United States presidential election in real time. The American nation reached election day on November 3, 2020, in the midst of two great uncertainties: the coronavirus pandemic and the information war over Republican or Democratic preferences. As we have already pointed out, uncertainty is the central link in the chain of formation of liquid risks. To get there, two processes have been interacting rapidly: the (globalized) complexity of the effects of the pandemic on the activity of the planet, including the impact on the economy and security of the United States; key aspects in the debate for power; and the incomprehension related to the nature of the virus, the effectiveness of the vaccines that were being developed at the time and the estimation of a date for the restart of activities in all areas, from industry to preschool education.

I remember being in Washington, DC, a week before the election. I was surprised to see the desolation looming in the streets, hundreds of closed places, and hotels operating at minimum capacity. It looked nothing like the capital of a country about to decide its political future for the next four years. We were in a reality where the future had become almost impossible to predict. On one hand, it was difficult to predict the election results. Both candidates presented themselves as equally strong or equally weak; the mainstream media seemed to support Joe Biden using surveys and historical data analysis as a basis. On the other hand, Donald Trump's rallies were packed with people despite the restrictions of the pandemic. There was simply not a system for comparing one candidate against the other because each band seemed to be manipulating the references. This ranged from the materialization of narratives to modify reality and history to the violation of weaknesses in electoral processes. Given that different electoral laws govern the states of the American nation and have several ways of choosing through in-person or mail votes, early votes, or voting on election day, an additional level of complexity was added. However, the most significant and paradoxical thing about the process was that all the available information was boosted into a vortex that, instead of informing, fulfilled the objective of misinforming. It was the perfect storm for a wide range of risks to unfold in all its liquidity. And so it was; the election occurred in such uncertainty that there were no definitive results for more than 30 days. A new level of misinformation began on the same night of November 3. Dozens of fraud allegations appeared supported by affidavits against Dominion, a company that provides voting technology. States such as Arizona, Pennsylvania, and Georgia could not declare a definitive winner, given the voting systems'; complexity and the closed results. More than a year after the 2020 election, there were still doubts upon its results, and about 30 percent of surveyed voters did not believe the process had been clean and transparent.

In an unprecedented action against the election results, Trump never officially recognized them nor granted Biden the victory. Instead, he decided to tour the country again and delegitimize the election. Despite such disconcerting behavior, even for some Republicans, a significant group of people continued supporting their candidate. It was not until January 6, 2021, that the unexpected occurred. In an even more liquid fusion of events, after a speech by President Trump in Washington DC, in which he insisted on the allegation of fraud being committed in the November 3rd elections and while the final certification of votes in Congress was taking place, a crowd of violent protesters took over the Capitol Building. This incident forced the suspension of the certification act, in which several Republican senators were initially determined to object to the process. The situation at the site reached a maximum point of uncontrollability, with five fatalities and dozens of injuries. Although Trump called for calm, outside the building, the digital social network "X"(previously known as Twitter) and other social networks decided to suspend president Trump's personal accounts, alleging his posts had encouraged insurrection and attacks against the rule of law. Once again, in a mix of narratives, truths, and perceptions, the violence that took place became the argument to delegitimize the allegations of fraud. From there, the president's defeat was consolidated, and he had to hand over his position two weeks later, as required by the Constitution.

In parallel, COVID-19 peaked in the United States on January 8, 2021, with 260,000 cases registered that day. The vaccine, which had generated enormous expectations, had begun to be applied in mid-December. However, it was an emergency operation, and the number of doses available was minimal for the date. All this added more anxiety and uncertainty to those two intense and liquid months. Between October 2020 and December 2020, a merge of political, social, and technological risks took place that had significant economic impacts. Thus, a fragment of recent history was useful to note the complex workings of liquid risks. Simultaneously, the evolution of multiple events accelerates, reality becomes complex and indecipherable, we enter the dynamics of uncertainty, and predicting the future becomes impossible.

4

Futurists of the present wanted

The future begins today, not tomorrow.

-John Paul II

A *Monday morning quarterback* is an American expression. It refers to the person who criticizes actions or decisions after their effects have materialized and there is sufficient evidence to evaluate reality. Obviously, in retrospect, the development of analysis and assessments is relatively easier, and the risk of failure is much lower. The challenge for anyone who intends to enter the world of liquid risks is to have foresight (and visibility of consequences). That is, seeing liquid risks in real-time, understanding the forces that interact in creating and developing these risks, and identifying their implications on the economic, social, political, and technological spheres (we should even add the moral sphere). Today, mastering this process constitutes one of the main security challenges for organizations and nations.

With the emergence of a widespread addiction to change, security references are being erased since many of them were the product of past experience. Therefore, the time has come to start looking for answers, paradoxical as it may seem, in the future. Undoubtedly, this phase of acceleration in which we live creates new security threats, some with deep and wide consequences. Even more so when we attempt to see the future with the canons of the past. An example is the concept widely used in crisis management, known as the worst-case scenario. Usually, it is defined as referencing the case with the greatest impact that occurred according to historical data. That is, protection systems should be able to tolerate conditions as severe as those experienced to date. However, reality shows that disasters will never be prevented entirely, and incidents will continue to escalate in magnitude. Let's look at the Fukushima nuclear power plant case in 2011. One of the design criteria for the plant was the possibility of resisting a magnitude nine earthquake. However, when the quake occurred, its builders realized it could not withstand the onslaught of the tsunami produced by the event. It had been such a large onslaught that was never estimated. Thus, although we may be aware that predicting the future is a serious challenge, we now have to assume that the past is no longer a valuable reference to face the magnitude and quality of the agents that propel the threats that this new logic and dynamic of the liquid brings with it. Even more so when the future accelerates and arrives at a speed that we do not expect. It is not about disqualifying and discarding the accumulated experience; on the contrary, it should be taken as the baseline in the upward curve and, from there, approach the future with an adaptive and flexible vision. The problem lies in the fact that the phenomena of globalization and technological acceleration are turning the world into a more complex and liquid thing by the hour. At the same time, security remains anchored in history, characterized by the permanent and the timeless. Although this is not bad, we need to understand that it is different and not enough. Change is happening now, and the time to act is now; not to do so is to fall far behind in the race.

The main obstacle to defining a secure future is disconnecting the static analysis of reality from the dynamic and mutating nature of the threats. We cannot approach the future thinking that tomorrow will be identical to today. The responsibilities of leaders in addressing operational issues are so high that they do not have the time or the energy needed to think about tomorrow. On the contrary, the elusiveness of the future makes them anxious and disarranges their compromised schemes of the present. Security has historically been built upon values, norms, compliance, justice, and even in God. However, at the fast pace movement of the world, reality becomes increasingly more complex, and individuals are left stripped of defenses. Even the concept of paradigm loses all its meaning in the accelerated transformation of liquid reality.

Let us examine Bitcoin, a cryptocurrency created by an anonymous individual (a.k.a. Satoshi Nakamoto), in 2009. Bitcoin was based on a new technology, the blockchain, which reconceptualized the meaning of trust. The blockchain is a distributed ledger that records all Bitcoin transactions. A network of computers maintains it, and no single entity controls it. The inherent decentralization in the blockchain means there is no need for a central bank or other authority to verify transactions. No government or central bank backs Bitcoin. Its value is determined by supply and demand. Bitcoin is a volatile asset. Its price can fluctuate wildly, and it is not suitable for everyone. However, it is a fascinating new technology with the potential to disrupt the financial system. Three of the leading cryptocurrencies: Bitcoin, Ethereum, and Ripple, have a combined market capitalization of over $1 trillion. This is equivalent to the sum of the GDP of several Latin American countries. Although the volatility of cryptocurrency values has been a major concern for investors, the market's growth suggests that cryptocurrencies have the potential to become a significant force in the global financial system. The expansion of the cryptocurrency market has been driven by a number of factors, including the increasing adoption of cryptocurrencies by businesses and institutions, the development of new cryptocurrency-based applications, and the growing awareness of the potential of cryptocurrencies. However, there are plenty of risks associated with them. One of its merits, decentralization, implies that no government regulates them, so there is no established institutional protection for investors. Additionally, cryptocurrencies are vulnerable to hacking and theft. Despite these structural risks, cryptocurrencies are a growing trend. They offer a new way to store and transfer value, and they have the potential to disrupt the traditional financial system. It will be interesting to see how cryptocurrencies develop in the future. We have gone, without even realizing it, from the solid economy of the gold standard (agreed in Bretton Woods, New Hampshire, in 1944) to an international monetary system that was made of pure fiat money (as of October 1976), to the virtualized economy of the digital tokens based on the blockchain technology. Therefore, it should not be a surprise to us that, in September 2021, China made cryptocurrencies illegal. Paradoxically, China was the country with the highest cryptocurrency mining activity in the World. In April 2021, China had 46% of the total, while the rest was spread across more than 30 countries.

Liquid risks are the inevitable consequence of two processes. On the one hand, from the acceleration of complexity, process driven by both technological development and globalization; on the other, from society's inability to absorb and process the pace of change (understanding its causes and consequences). It is in the gap of ignorance about this process where new and powerful threats live and multiply. A risk is liquid because its shape mutates and adapts to the environment. It is difficult to contain; it spills easily, and although it is intangible when determined with any degree of precision, its effects can be very real. These liquid risks have begun to manifest themselves in multiple ways. Two of these ways are the increase in political instability and polarization. For example, China is one of the poles of attraction capable of altering the world's risk profile in real time. In 2014, the Chinese government decided to move an oil drilling platform off the coast of Vietnam, sparking anti-Chinese protests in Ho Chi Minh City and forcing the closure of several global toy and clothing manufacturing plants. This is how a conflict over territorial waters in Southeast Asia emptied the shelves of some chain stores in the United States a few weeks later. Another case involves the Evergreen supercargo ship, which ran aground in the Suez Canal in March 2021 and blocked world trade for several days, with an estimated impact on losses of 0.4% of world trade and around 145,000 mentions on "X" are proof of the degree of interdependence and connectivity in which we live daily.

With COVID-19, the horrible pandemic that began at the end of 2019 in Wuhan, China, the global power of liquid risks became evident. As of December 2021, the pandemic had caused 5.42 million deaths worldwide (although the numbers are deemed to be higher). Realities are no longer limited to the local; they are transmitted rapidly and become global. This happens with viruses but goes much further; it applies equally to terrorism, cyberattacks, asymmetric wars, and even fake news. Another manifestation of the power of liquid risks is seen in the increasing difficulty organizations have in maintaining secrets. This is because the connectivity of networks and the horizontality of power have led interest groups to demand, more forcefully, information about the direction of trends. At the same time, people become virtualized and produce multiple versions of their reality. The question remains: Who is who behind the networks? Who to trust? At the same time we are asking for transparency in the collective we seem to be willing to accept more opaque and diffuse behaviors in the individual.

An additional example of liquid risk is found in what has been labeled alternative truth. These are, in essence, distorted versions of the objective facts of reality that generally seek to hide or disguise lies. Alternative truths are well constructed; they take concrete and proven facts to develop highly convincing arguments aimed at moving public opinion in the direction of usually obscure or biased objectives. The main difficulty in neutralizing an alternative truth is that its origin are fallacious arguments that use complex structures such as the media, prestigious personalities, and large budgets to sustain themselves. But what is the interest in promoting and maintaining false stories? And who profits from them? The purpose is essentially political-economic. To visualize it, you must understand how the globalized world operates and the value of information in the high-level decision-making process. The alternative truth is not intended to be a prophecy that, by spreading so much, ends up self-fulfilling. It is about constructing a parallel narrative subjected to reality only through specific facts. It is promoted as an irrefutable truth through multiple means, even if the evidence demonstrates the opposite.

Liquid risks are to security, what the ipod was to music at the time. Those who understood the change adapted and made the leap to a different dimension; under new paradigms and with other rules, they were successful and survived; those who did not anticipate the changes remained tied to the past as if standing on a worthless format, inadequate to a new reality that made them disappear. Let us look at the stumbles and fall of Kodak in 2012, the giant photography corporation, because its management could not foresee the evolution in digital image capture and transmission. This is the challenge: making the unknown conscious, increasing the pace of understanding the environment by immersing yourself in it instead of isolating yourself, and adapting flexibly to the situations that the accelerated future brings you. Additionally, security must assume a strategic role within the organization it serves while being able to automate repetitive operational processes. This is a migration towards intelligence, the construction of powerful alliances, and the development of processes that analyze scenarios and consequences of the decisions made in the present. In this era of liquid risks, there will never be enough security. For this reason, we should design prospective rather than retrospective solutions, capable of better reading the future ahead since that is where we will encounter the dangers with the power to affect us. The new challenges for global security involve understanding the complexity of the new realities and, from there, designing flexible structures with leadership capable of adapting to changes and knowing how to transform uncertainties into certainties. In the end, the liquid world seems to be reminding us that there is not a more complicated challenge than predicting the future. However, we have to assume that the past is no longer a sufficient reference to face the magnitude and quality of the agents that propel the threats that this new dynamic of the liquid brings with it, even more so when the future accelerates and arrives at a speed that we do not expect.

5

We come from chaos, and towards chaos, we go

We do not want changes. All change constitutes a threat to stability.

-Aldous Huxley, Brave New World

I n its most basic form, risk is the sum of threats and vulnerabilities. Vulnerabilities can be considered weaknesses or flaws through which threats can penetrate and exploit, thus materializing a risk. Every materialized risk entails a loss, which is neither always material nor susceptible to being expressed in terms of money. We can also lose time, reputation, health, lives, and market, among others. If we refer to liquid risks, we must be aware that the differentiating factor with respect to the nature of other risks is that their causes are also liquid, regardless of whether these are vulnerabilities or threats. Therefore, we find that most liquid risks are the product of liquid threats that begin by exploiting the same vulnerability: the ignorance that individuals, organizations and societies have about the accelerated pace of change that occurs in our environment. This accelerated change manifests itself in multiple ways, from the institutional fragility of democracy, given the rigidity of its patterns, to how malleable the individual's decision-making power has become through social networks. The actors behind these liquid threats are varied and usually not easily revealed. On the contrary, they infiltrate or hide behind everyday life, institutions and the truth. It seems paradoxical that, despite the unprecedented technological boom and hyperconnectivity, present day threats are more anonymous, ubiquitous, and unpredictable than ever before. They are so because of their agents' power and skill in managing the advantages offered by the knowledge and information society.

There are multiple threats that do not have a permanent physical materiality or that live camouflaged in the environment. Today, a part of terrorism occurs in the media sphere. The generation and spread (like viruses) of false or conspiratorial narratives are frequently aimed at demoralizing the population. People become sick with hopelessness and, more often than not, the enemy wins the battle without the need to fight on the physical plane.

The diminished capabilities that nation States have to protect their citizens against these enhanced dangers have been evidenced in the dozens of terrorist attacks that have occurred in recent years in Europe and America. On July 14, 2016, a lone attacker of Tunisian citizenship, driving a cargo vehicle, rammed into hundreds of people on the Promenade in Nice when they were celebrating France's Independence Day, leaving 84 dead. One of the reasons that explain the limited evolution of security in recent years is linked to the few complications that authorities have had in the recent past in identifying, reading, and interpreting the level of danger that threats had. When the characteristics and motivations of present-day threats are examined, regardless of their origin or nature, it is possible to identify some features that distinguish them but, at the same time, make them more complex to combat and neutralize. Not all of these features are expressed with equal intensity or magnitude in each threat, and their ability to mutate in time, space, and modes of operation in order to maintain, in some cases, the anonymity or low profile of their adventures should not be ignored. Below the main characteristics of the threats.

1. Construction of networks

Organized crime, fundamentalist terrorism, or xenophobic groups do not act like people with recognizable faces. On the contrary, they are intricate organizations with matrix structures associated with functions and regions in which work is segmented and articulated so that everyone depends on everyone in a distributed engineering model, which carefully fragments information and power. It is a mesh with multiple interaction nodes in which the collective prevails over the individual. For example, drug cartels simultaneously operate cultivation, procurement, production, distribution, and marketing processes in specialized chains that extend throughout the world, where only very few have a global vision of the business. Hence, there is an extreme difficulty in completely dismantling these organizations.

2. Connection with power

Behind the criminal activities of sophisticated and complex levels of organization, vast amounts of money are moved that are used to bribe and extort the weakened institutions of corrupt States from which these new threats take advantage to position themselves strategically, in the decision-making layers of the power structures. However, in the case of terrorist networks, the power established through institutions is not an end in itself but rather represents an objective that must be subverted, trying to strengthen its bases, exposing its weaknesses and contradictions to generate unrest in the citizen, who observes how States cannot, effectively, confront manifestations of violence and cruelty typical of these movements. With some frequency, the Colombian guerrilla carries out attacks on civilian populations in provinces where the army is unable to have a presence, producing frustration in the population, who are usually unable to perceive the government's action. Similarly, groups of cybercriminals penetrate, attack, and take control of information networks of government agencies with the sole objective of weakening the institutions on which the constituted and formal power resides.

3.   Empowerment through chaos

Frequently these new threats capitalize on social entropy for their benefit. It is a very common feature in criminal networks. Hence, their interest in subverting the established order, generating uncertainty, and dislocating the structures that support or enforce the rules. As the energy of chaos is highly destabilizing, merging with it leads to scenarios of anarchy, which are conducive to spreading organized networks of evil.

The gray areas

Liquid threats have a unique ability to dissolve structures and institutions. When States are fragile, sovereignty is one of their objectives. The dissolution of sovereignty manifests itself in multiple ways, but perhaps the most obvious is what occurs at borders. It is around the edges where countries fray. This does not happen by chance, and generally, these are processes that lead to conflicts. When a government destroys institutions, it turns impunity into a bonus for the criminal. At the same time, that government becomes the main threat to its population. If it also divides the territory into lots that can be exploited by criminal activity, then we are faced with the logic of the dissolution of a nation, expressed in the acceleration of conflict in multiple social layers. This becomes more evident with the strengthening of criminal groups that may be ideologically close to the government or that are simply convenient to the State because they deliver funds whose origin and destination it does not have to account for because the State considers it is money extra-state or parastatals. Another critical aspect of the complexity present in borders is the non-linearity of reality. This refers to the fact that in the vicinity of the borders, there is no direct relationship between causes and consequences; everything is vague and nebulous (typical of gray areas). Hence, there is difficulty in understanding what is happening and the ease with which new conflicts can occur.

Crime is always present and opportunistic. When the conditions are met, a structure as a criminal gang will change from low-intensity states to more and better organized and self-sustaining organizational forms. Hence, the deinstitutionalization of the State is directly proportional to the expansion of organized crime. At higher levels, criminal structures not only expand but exercise their authority above what may remain of the State and its population. This is the so-called criminal peace, a complex form of order within chaos that is based on fear and repression. However, as in any complex system, crime operates far from its equilibrium point at these magnitudes. However, it is adaptive and very sensitive to environmental conditions. This means that societies always live at some point on the continuum between the two extremes: negotiation and conflict. These are systems that need conflict to channel the energies of crime. For this reason, the criminal prefers gray and chaotic environments, and if there is any peace, it is imposed by crime, always dependent on the random will of the boss on duty. Once societies enter the complex dynamics of chaos, any reference system based on institutionality disappears. There are no longer fixed parameters, and it is precisely in that state that it is easier to dominate people.

These new threats are no longer limited to Islamist groups or transnational organized crime. The political crises of representative democracy, as we know it today, have been incubating a type of risk increasingly present in the West. It is about the access to power of populist or ultra-nationalist leaders and movements through electoral processes. In the 2021 German elections, the Alliance for

Germany (AfD) party won 10.3% of the votes, and around 4.8 million people supported it. This organization was founded in 2013 with a conservative affiliation between the right and the extreme right. Its populist ideology defends nationalist proposals; it defines itself as eurosceptic, and its project is to unlink the country from the Euro and restore the German Mark. In the same way, the Catalan separatist movement held a referendum to demonstrate that its territory is not part of the Spanish kingdom. Added to these demonstrations are the controversial 2020 elections in the United States, the victory of Brexit in England, and other polarizing trends that seem to mark a different step in the world's geopolitics. Although each nation has its right to self-determination and these processes have been taking place within the democratic electoral order, what we are beginning to see should alert us in assessing potential new threats that are foreshadowed. We are not facing a natural process of progress. It is becoming increasingly evident that there is a segregation strategy that may empower certain elites while isolating large portions of the population, whether by race, origin, religion, or immigration status, seeking to impose a single personified model of thought by some privileged people in a sort of historical vindication. It is a formula that works differently in each country but has the same objective: the alleged defense of society from the risks of globalization and the integration of the world. It is a paradox that these movements arise from the same sources that three decades ago, after the fall of the Berlin Wall, promoted a universal dynamic of integration, free trade, and democratization. The actors behind these sources have now decided that the evils of humanity were a product of an overfusion and that it must be reversed to begin to address the problems. The expressions of these threats range from turning migrant caravans into pieces of social artillery aimed at manipulating and generating tension in overloaded institutions to encourage separatist groups that foster polarization based on the loss of identity with a continent or a country. This is the way that scenarios that we had deemed outdated are now reappearing. For example, the leader of a nation may openly threaten the use of atomic weapons; human beings, by the millions, will have to leave their countries because their parents were not born in the same land; borders that had been open for decades are suddenly closed; and opponents are persecuted or perpetually imprisoned for crimes linked to the way of thinking. Thus, to maintain a minimum level of security, States are challenged to fight fiercely against crimes protected by society's liquidity while taking care of the thin and sometimes blurred line of Human Rights.

In the liquid world, norms and values have lost the sense of permanence once characteristic of immovable and solid justice. In reducing liquid threats, it is worth asking: how can we contain justice in the territoriality of States when the criminals are globalized nomads? Battles against crime today have no borders and, in many cases, are not even subject to space-time dimensions. Therefore, jurisdiction in the exercise of law ends up fading in the intricate networks populated by people whom we only know by their avatars and who, equipped with the ubiquity of technology, appear and disappear in the instantaneousness of liquid modernity.

There are other new and liquid threats that have spillover because of a generalized lack of understanding of societies that have globalized at an accelerated pace. Some had very specific objectives and high destruction power. We refer, for example, to the systematic generation of uncertainty through complexity, the manipulation of electoral systems, or the use of biometric surveillance, Artificial Intelligence tools, and big data for social control. Authoritarian or dictatorial regimes do not only use advanced technological means to control their citizens. There are several, and increasingly frequent, governments in States with a democratic tradition that use this technological fusion of processing and storage capacity for purposes beyond State intelligence. Through them, profiles are built on ideological orientations, consumption habits, sexual preferences, and many other characteristics to broadcast powerful personalized messages able to induce specific behaviors or decisions. This is what we saw in 2016, with Cambridge Analytica and the election of Donald Trump in the United States, in the Brexit referendum in the United Kingdom, and during the pandemic, with the issuance of a Green Pass in Europe created with the intention of segmenting citizens based on their beliefs regarding the COVID-19 vaccine.

Liquid risks are derived from liquid threats which, as we already mentioned, result from the lack of understanding of the environment caused by the acceleration of globalization and technology. Being unable to understand the phenomena surrounding us is equivalent to being lost. Not knowing where we are is when we are most vulnerable hence, the increased risk we all now face of becoming victims. The problem with liquid risks is that, unlike other categories of risks, whose effects we feel immediately, this new class of risks, because they are diffuse or diluted, we are prone to accept them without being aware that we expose ourselves to losing assets much more valuable than money. And here, we are referring to freedom, privacy, or the possibility of choosing.

What is not known cannot be estimated.

6

The Conquest of uncertainty

It is the uncertainty that enchants us;
everything becomes wonderful in the mist.

-Fyodor Dostoyevsky

Uncertainty is the first product of the interaction between accelerationism and complexity and lies at the center of the formation cycle of liquid risks. Therefore, we should learn to live (and deal) with it because it has become an inherent part of our lives. Human beings are generally attracted to certainty and order. Chaos scenarios force a permanent adaptation that is resource-consuming, placing at risk achieved goals. Although since we appeared on Earth, we have faced all kinds of vicissitudes, we have achieved our most important advances during periods of relative peace, which are determined in part by the predictability of events. Due to the need for stability inherent to the individual, uncertainty has become synonymous with insecurity. This is the main reason why individuals in contemporary society want to live in areas of certainty. However, at the same time, our society has created the addictive rush of accelerated complexity (as if we would be looking all the time at a rush to the head of adrenaline, dopamine, and serotonin). Life between these two irreconcilable terrains is, in some way, the cause of an existential anguish filled with complexities and simultaneity. Thus, the cost of living in this liquid world is paid by trading certainties for uncertainty.

Being prisoners of the certainty-uncertainty dilemma is equivalent to living subject to the relativism that engenders chaos, which, for the purposes of the liquid world, we could define as a state in which the logical relationships of cause and effect are fractured, and society loses the stability necessary for development. It ends up investing more energy in survival than in individual and collective objectives and aspirations. It is a very sophisticated trap of the unconscious since we can believe we are running rapidly toward progress when we are actually moving to survival. Certainties are not necessarily truths. For example, although we can be convinced that the Sun moves from East to West in the sky, the truth is that the Sun is motionless with respect to the Earth, and we are the ones who rotate. Certainties, therefore, are built on frames of reference and perceptions and not only on facts. We have tried to make certainties a goal that, once achieved, should never be lost. However, not all certainties are tangible; in many cases, they are the opposite: uncertainty is absolute. In these times of volatility, ambiguity, and acceleration of complexity, we will most likely live without any certainty. Furthermore, we have turned uncertainty into a taboo, a bad word, something to be avoided and hated. Uncertainty has no measure. What is not known cannot be estimated, and in the canons of the static world, approaching it produces the fear of leaving what is safe. The problem is that, just as we have no control over uncertainty, we also have no control over certainties, given their dependence on referential frameworks and perceptions. One place where we will always find uncertainty is in the future. In it, the anxieties and fears of the unknown and the unexpected are combined. The future frames a fluid relativism where nothing is sustained, according to the dynamics of the aversion to what is permanent.

Although there is no formula to successfully face uncertainty, deal with it, and manage it, so to speak, doing so is one of the most demanding challenges for leadership. It is the leader to whom everyone turns in search of answers when the perspective seems uncertain. Thus, managing uncertainty becomes an exploitable field full of opportunities for those capable of making their way through complexity. To be successful in this endeavor, it is desirable to develop some particular skills, including constructing images that draw a better future despite the present-time adversities. Even in scenarios of maximum shock, patterns appear that establish specific rules and, somehow, make reality worth living. For security, it is essential to identify and study these zones of certainty or stability since they contain keys to addressing aspects such as the sustainability of spaces of peace and order imbued in chaotic environments and managing adversity in communities highly impacted by the loss of social predictability.

However, it is unhealthy to invent certainties that explain uncertainty or formulate arguments that reveal the unknown, pressured by the natural anxiety of not being able to bear knowing what is to come. The spaces managed to conquer uncertainty do not necessarily, nor immediately, transform into certainties. A void of uncertainty may occur, waiting to be filled by answers under construction. Creating plans to emerge from a deep crisis is a good example. We can have an excellent situational diagnosis of the causes and even manage to identify the objectives to achieve to overcome the contingencies. However, the generation of agreements, the definition of the direction towards which it is necessary to begin to move, and the production of the momentum necessary for the change to take place are, in principle, spaces of uncertainty with high levels of complexity. We have colonized spaces of uncertainty that have not yet been transformed into certainties.

Facing uncertainty with a fast response and flexibility is advisable. Approaching uncertainty with schemes that are too rigid or with extreme caution can be counterproductive. Although science has methodological answers for research, agile exploration, in the form of terrain recognition, initially allows us to delve into the unknown. It is about moving forward without many preconceived ideas but with the intention of tracing a route of movement that encompasses the greatest number of variables and the way in which they interact, placing at the higher levels of the causal hierarchy those that seem to have greater weight or power of influence. Once these first forces that define the scenario have been identified, some initial models or working hypotheses that attempt to predict future situations can be built.

———————————— O ————————————

Urban space as a factor of transformation and social order is a good example of uncertainty management. An environmental design trend that is gaining allies and is now common in highly congested cities is that instead of building new streets and highways, cities are adopting policies for the development of pedestrian-only spaces equipped with public transportation. What may initially seem like an action against all logic results in the humanization of the public space.

In the face of traffic chaos, citizens who travel by alternative means on safer boulevards prevail. Some cities have opted to reduce the number of private vehicles that enter their perimeters, charging them higher toll rates and increasing the cost of parking. In contrast, the rates of the public transportation system are reduced or subsidized to encourage citizens to use the system. Rethinking urban mobility as another variable to reduce chaos and insecurity is a skillful incentive management formula that translates into high-impact public policies.

Another aspect worth mentioning is the ability of communities (in a sort of bottom-up process) to organize themselves in networks to better deal with the dynamics of chaos. In this sense, social cohesion is a new variable proposed to respond to uncertainty-related threats. Socially cohesive communities are characterized by a global situation in which their citizens share a sense of belonging and inclusion, actively participate in public affairs, recognize and tolerate differences, enjoy relative equity in access to goods and services, and regarding the distribution of income and wealth. All this is in an environment of relative certainty, where institutions generate trust and legitimacy. As a complement, uncertainty management needs a leadership capable of challenging the status quo. Perhaps the motivating element to face the uncertainty is to leave the stable and well-ordered regions built around certainties. While certainties are not a permanent guarantee of security or stability, it is natural to prefer them to the darkness of ignorance. But as we have already mentioned, in the liquid and complex realities, the areas of certainty change rapidly, and after the change, uncertainty arises.

We should always choose to deal with uncertainty as a team. This is because, more often than not, a single head or a pair of hands is not enough in the face of the unexplored. The challenge of uncertainty requires a team of courageous problem solvers with an appetite for risk. A diverse group inspired by doubts, willing to state questions rather than answers and with the ability to enjoy the adrenaline of discovery, dissatisfied people, willing to confront this sea monster that is uncertain with arguments but also a team of people who are capable of acknowledging the achievements of their fellows. A delicate combination of provocateurs with conciliators and inspirational with pragmatists. Leaders and organizations today have the unavoidable responsibility of building certainties. The spaces of certainty in the midst of uncertainty make the complex reality derived from chaos more livable. If we know anything, it is that in adverse times, people follow those who project hope for the future and those capable of transmitting certainties and managing uncertainty. It is a necessary reflection in the face of a complex, accelerating future.

In complex environments, strategies designed with few margins of flexibility usually fail. Too many destabilizing forces coexist, from which new difficulties and possibilities emerge.

7

Walking the tightrope of complexity

The more I see, the less I know for sure.

-John Lennon

I f we were to compare liquid risks to a piece of fabric, its threads would represent the complexity. Complex systems are a tapestry of variables, each acting simultaneously and interwoven in a perpetual dance. What's intriguing is that these variables don't nullify each other. Instead, they often amplify or complement one another. These variables, or forces, don't require consensus to influence reality; each acts according to its own interests and motivations. In complexity, the system's components operate with local information. This means decisions are made based on personal beliefs, positions, history, and resources without universal agreement. It's akin to the neurons in the human brain, each performing its function, but together, creating consciousness.

Complex realities usually defy conventional logic. In turbulent times, cause-effect relationships are no longer direct or linear, which is why it is challenging to fit ideas and reasoning from the past to be consistent with our limited ability to understand the liquid environment. The world around us, being complex, does not allow us to dismantle it, simplify it, and address it in parts. By doing so, we modify it, which leads to falsifying the analysis and reaching erroneous conclusions. It is, in a sense, the relativistic paradox of the observer who, by observing, modifies what is observed. This is so because, in complexity, the elements are arranged to operate under specific parameters of self-organization and with emergent properties (new capabilities that arise spontaneously to adapt to changes in the environment). More clearly, it is a network of variables whose joint action is much greater than the sum of its parts, although there are no prior agreements between them. A system with emergent properties is in constant movement; it does not limit itself because doing so would weaken it. Since it has to build possibilities on the fly to survive, adapt, or advance. Therefore, it cannot be closed. On the contrary, it is open to its environment and is extremely sensitive to changes around it. In complex environments, rigid strategies or strategies designed with few margins of flexibility usually fail. Too many destabilizing forces coexist in these liquid realities, from which new difficulties and possibilities emerge.

Only in environments with low levels of uncertainty is it possible to extrapolate or project a given reality. In the world of liquid risks, we can predict the near future with low probabilities. We do not live in linearity or proportionality; small changes can produce unimaginable consequences. This is because complexity is in continuous imbalance, and what is imbalanced produces gradients that cause everything to move in an attempt to stabilize. Still, since so many varied forces are present, the system never reaches a position of rest. Hence, Bauman's reflection:

"What was once a lifelong project has today become an attribute of the moment. Once designed, the future is not forever but needs to be continually assembled and disassembled. Apparently contradictory, each of these two operations has comparable importance and tends to be equally absorbing."

Complex systems are closely linked to their history and, to some extent, determine them. This means that reality does not occur by chance of the moment but rather takes the past into consideration. As everything flows rapidly, history also accelerates, filling itself with a sequence of realities that, although they may seem incomprehensible, are not discontinuous. The problem is that liquid risks are formed in complexity and are the consequence of the accelerationism in which we are immersed, so there is no way to avoid them.

Those with security management responsibilities today must embrace complexity and integrate the ability to analyze it into a portfolio of critical competencies. Failure to do so would lead to continuing to see a closed and static world. In summary, the challenge of understanding complexity is linked to seven properties:

1. They are open systems where it is difficult to define which elements are directly part of the system and which are part of the environment. Depending on their dynamics, sometimes the systems temporarily integrate parts that are not their own. Therefore, it is hard to classify the liquid risks into a single category. Since they are open, they overlap each other and form new risks.

2. Complexity develops in a space of nonlinear relationships. This means the connections between causes and consequences are not obvious, direct, or inversely proportional. Significant phenomena may not affect the system, while imperceptible variations can completely transform it. Hence, the difficulty in analyzing the impact on liquid risks. However, nonlinearity has an additional component: given the very high sensitivity of the system, it is impossible to rule out forces, no matter how small they might be.

3. Complex realities have very low predictability because many interactions occur in them. Those interactions are imperceptible at a micro level and, when combined rapidly, are enhanced, generating unexpected changes known as emergent phenomena. In risk analysis, everything that is emergent is unknown. Therefore, it isn't easy to estimate its consequences.

4. Complex systems have the property of self-organizing. This characteristic allows them to sustain themselves, even if their parts are not entirely aligned or in agreement. Self-organization occurs because each element profits from the system's activity as a whole, successfully exercising its purpose. One way of looking at it is that, in complexity, an authority is not needed to tell others what to do. It is enough for each system member to know the purpose and contribute individually towards achieving the common objective. Seen from liquid risks, self-organization is a property well exploited by threat generators. Among these actors, the common purpose is maximizing their profits (and objectives) with the least possible exposure; hence, in the liquid world, threats become anonymous and are difficult to trace.

5. Complex systems are adaptable. This allows them to overcome environmental adversities. Adaptability is one of the easiest properties to recognize in these systems; although not all complexity is equally adaptable, the complex systems that make up the liquid world are. Adaptive capacity allows them to change shape and modify their functionality without losing focus on their purpose. Hence, liquid risks are an expression of complex environments. Just as reality becomes blurred and less predictable, the risks that inhabit it assimilate similar properties, becoming more challenging to identify and, therefore, to mitigate.

6. Complexity implies an inherent difficulty in explaining or reducing to simple concepts. Complex systems can only be approached from multiple legitimate perspectives to define them in all their dimensions. Because of this attribute, the complex resists being accommodated to concepts of the solid and linear world.

7. Complex systems cannot be reduced to simpler scales. This fractal property of complexity means that regardless of the dimension or part of the system we study, it will always be complex.

Mass migrations

One way to understand complexity is to observe and analyze some phenomena of the liquid world in which we live. A dramatic and authentic example is the recent surge of mass migrations. They can be forced by armed conflicts, deterioration of the economies in the countries, or for political reasons. Recently, I have been closely involved in studying and understanding the complexity of the migrations of millions of Venezuelans who have left their country. According to the Regional Interagency Coordination Platform for Refugees and Migrants of Venezuela (Platform R4V), led by UNHCR and IOM, as of August 2023, the outflow of refugees and migrants from Venezuela, deemed to be the largest displacement crisis in the world, had reached 7.7 million migrants and refugees. Mass migrations from Venezuela began in 2015, and as of the registration date, more than 20 percent of the population had left the country. This is the largest migratory movement recorded on the American continent and the second largest after that, produced by the war in Syria. To understand the dimensions of Venezuelan migration, it is enough to say that in proportion, it would be equivalent in the United States to the entire population of California and Florida. However, the complexity of the Venezuelan migration phenomenon does not only come from the number of people crossing the borders, most of them to Colombia. The effect is enhanced when it is appreciated that behind each migrant remains a family in which a void is generated that is impossible to fill. At the same time, social and economic pressure is produced on the countries receiving the migration. These elements have non-linear effects, both in Venezuela and in the States that accept the migrants.

The fact that a productive member of a household stops contributing resources to the family while, amid uncertainty, she manages to generate money to send as a remittance produces an immediate deterioration in the living conditions of her environment, in addition to the emotional and psychological emotions activated by the absence of loved ones. In parallel, the majority of countries that receive migration already live on the edge of citizen demands, so they are not prepared to absorb masses of the population that need attention, thus creating severe service crises, manifestations of xenophobia, and other disorders, usually disproportionate in comparison to the number of migrants.

An additional component of complexity in the case of Venezuelan migration is that, in some way, migratory movements are caused by action or omission. The deterioration of living conditions within the country is a consequence of institutional destruction, repression, and social control, all factors that change the relationship of incentives of the population, who prefer to risk leaving in search of improving their situation and that of their loved ones, rather than remaining in uncertainty and the accelerated deterioration of their environment.

The common Venezuelan does not need to exhaustively evaluate or build a consensus on migrating. Migrants make their choices based on local information, considering their circumstances, vision, and interests. However, it is impressive that with poor coordination and communication, a consensus seems to emerge among millions of migrants regarding the decision to leave the country for good through the borders. A characteristic of the phenomena that complexity creates is the capacity for self-organization among the system's many elements to become sustainable. That is to say, several activities, forces, and trends arise (emerge), both licit and illicit, that turn migration into a big business.

Among the emerging phenomena are many initiatives, motivations of individuals and organizations to support migrants, NGOs defending migrant rights, humanitarian aid, and agreements for the regularization of immigration status, but human and drug trafficking also appear, sexual exploitation, child labor, and other forms of slavery. In this broad spectrum of phenomena, one of the most complex liquid risks to understand emerges: the use of mass migrations as a weapon in new wars.

In 2018, a record number of 400,000 people were captured trying to enter the United States illegally. In October of that year, a caravan of seven thousand migrants arrived at Mexico's southern border, mainly from Honduras, El Salvador, and Guatemala. To date, it is the largest organized group ever seen, with declared intentions of reaching and entering North American countries. In Intelligence investigations carried out in Guatemala, it was evident that this caravan had been financed with funds contributed from Venezuela and was intended to generate destabilization and chaos in the United States. The caravan also constituted itself as a form of protest against immigration policies and the changes in asylum laws imposed by Donald Trump.

More recently and as a form of organized crime, human trafficking mafias, in complicity with officials of the Venezuelan Identification and Immigration Service, have established networks to send migrants willing to cross the southern border to the United States and seek asylum or temporary protection policies.

Migratory movements as an example of complexity serve well to understand the imbalances between borders, even more so when there is such a gap in the quality of life between both sides of a strip, which marks the pressure gradient between one side and the other and what stimulates the unstoppable flow of people who by any means try to leave Venezuela. Mass migrations, in addition to being intrinsically complex, are now weapons of political action in new wars. In November 2021, Elizabeth Braw, a senior fellow specializing in gray zone advocacy at the American Enterprise Institute—a business freedom-oriented think tank—wrote regarding migration as weapons of war:

"This is where Lukashenko's sinister game gets even smarter. The Belarusian leader knows that immigration is a very divisive issue within the European Union and individually between its member states. Poland's strategy of returning migrants to Belarus has already caused a rift with Brussels and thus worsened Poland's already strained relations with the EU headquarters. In fact, Lukashenko knew that migrants forced by his regime to go to Latvia, Lithuania, and Poland were unlikely to stay there. In September and October, German police registered 7,300 migrants arriving in Germany through Poland and Belarus. This sudden influx of migrants, in turn, has caused far-right German activists to travel to the border to try to keep them away."

The complex phenomenon of mass migration is now globalizing, and it is no coincidence that it attacks Colombia, the United States, and Poland simultaneously. It is a liquid risk that is planned, both by countries with dictatorial regimes and by nations with a democratic tradition, and its purpose is to destabilize and soften the legitimacy of republics with sovereign visions of their democracies.

The price we pay for being part of this global digital community is the amount of data we give up.

8

Hansel and Gretel with algorithms

The complexity is free.

-Thomas Friedman

In his work Introduction to Complex Thinking, the French philosopher and sociologist Edgar Morin (1921) points out that the most serious threats facing humanity are linked to the blind and uncontrolled progress of knowledge, mainly because of the mutilating way in which knowledge is organized, incapable of recognizing and encompassing the complexity of reality. Today, it is clear that the problem is not availability or rapid access to data. The physics of semiconductors has continuously lowered the costs of storing information while the speed of microprocessors increases at a geometric rate. Morin refers to the selection and ranking of data considered significant over others assumed to be secondary, leaving out large amounts of uninterpreted information and, therefore, discarded or suspended, awaiting a search under other criteria.

Another critical aspect is the scientific validation bias intended to be given to the information. During the past COVID-19 pandemic, the a priori disqualification of figures, medications, and origins of the virus became common, which, because an elite did not endorse them, were censored or canceled in the mainstream media or on social networks and then reappeared as data certified by the same elites when veracity, effectiveness or value were proven as elements of a particular narrative. This occurred when the Chinese authorities insisted that there was no evidence of virus transmission among humans and, in other situations, such as the use of face masks, the application of booster doses of vaccines, or the numbers needed to reach herd immunity.

Scientific validation, although necessary, becomes a liquid risk when political or economic agendas mediate it or respond to the interests of power. What is relevant is that in the face of this explosion in information processing and storage capabilities, the increasingly sophisticated algorithms of AI and Deep Learning have begun to discover infinite correlations in data that, until very recently, succumbed to the forgotten. It is worth saying, however, that all this power is insufficient if an additional skill is lacking: the understanding and synthesis that contain some meaning to interpret that reality. Edgar Morin's thesis is still valid; the acceleration of the complex increases, and the gap between human understanding and the actual reality (to distinguish it in some way from what we believe to be reality or perceived reality) widens. It is an unprecedented expansion in history and seems to be progressively covering everything. So many options open up with each new technological impulse that there is no way to contain or classify the amount of information at the accelerated speed at which it is generated. Thus, diversity gives rise to information bubbles in which only fanatics of highly specialized knowledge coexist.

Suppose you are a fan of cameras from the 60s of the 20th century. In a simple Internet search, you can get millions of links and hundreds of thousands of people with the same tastes almost anywhere in the world who have forums, online sales, and photography courses 24 hours a day. Together, they have built a larger and more active community than many countries' populations, in which they interact in permanent feedback cycles, which makes them even more specialized. Learning curves have become shorter and steeper due to these accelerated dynamics of information and knowledge. In fact, there were cult cameras launched on the market during the 1960s, such as the Nikon F, the Leica M4, and the Kodak Instamatic 100. The latter, introduced to the market in 1963, was a precursor to the massification of photography due to the simplicity of its operation. Kodak marketing researchers have already identified the need for a camera to capture those fleeting moments quickly and cheaply.

The exciting thing is that the example suggests that in the 60s, there was an attempt to capture the moment. But that is unrelated to the emergence of global digital communities of people with specialized interests. However, not all virtual communities on the web dedicate thousands of hours to a healthy exploration of culture or hobbies. The problem arises when similar communities coalesce around innovation in terrorism, sexual exploitation of children, or the development of synthetic drugs. We cannot ignore the fact that technologies enable the individual's potential, and if rules and controls are not established, they will gain fertile and lucrative terrain in the dark networks of crime. Although this is not new, nor should it surprise us, what does constitute a risk is the acceleration of the gap between the capabilities that criminal networks have to create gray zones and thus cause harm and the response of institutional and judicial forces to neutralize them.

Technological advantages not only empower lone wolf criminals operating behind computer barriers that make them invisible. Also, authoritarian regimes take advantage of various tools aimed at listening to and intervening in communications, producing fake news with high dissemination power, and carrying out selective internet blocking to censor media critical of the actions of these governments. The power of these new threats is no longer just in anonymity. Their capabilities have expanded as fast as technology, and they have some additional advantages, such as using cryptocurrencies to finance and globalize their activities. We see that in the same great complexity market accelerated by technology, all kinds of threats are supplied without significant distinctions between what represents a benefit or a danger. This liquefaction of limits is, in itself, the characterization of liquid risk. It is a reality built on addiction to change, difficult to define or contain, but with devastating effects.

In January 2018, Google recognized that trends could emerge in its algorithms based on search patterns. Although they warned that they did not intend to be arbiters of the truth, even less so on controversial issues such as climate change, they indicated at the time that they were working to present balanced information. This all arises because in 2017, after the election of Donald Trump, the term filter bubble reappeared. Author and internet activist Eli Pariser coined it in his 2011 book, The Filter Bubble, where Pariser describes how search algorithms are based on the user's previous searches and preferences that people leave in their online browsing to create profiles and thus form large bubbles of information within which they group many other related profiles. Pariser's thesis has been discussed, supported, or refuted. However, the truth is that evidence suggests that bubbles exist, and, as has been suggested, they accentuate polarization by experts and data analysts such as Bill Gates or Sir Tim Berners Lee, especially on political issues. Liquid risk is not only the bias in knowledge that can arise but also manipulation through false information, the exploitation of certain weaknesses associated with specific profiles for marketing purposes, and social control through certain types of information curated to specific audiences. As usually happens in the liquid world, cause-effect relationships are not linear, and this causes paradoxes to arise. In this case, technological acceleration has broken down the borders in individuals' connectivity, erasing space-time restrictions. In parallel, it has created bubbles of knowledge that keep people confined within a kind of information silos that isolates them from other realities and interests.

Returning to Edgar Morin, the reductionist need to fragment knowledge to supposedly understand better does not lead to an accurate analysis since we have reached a point where complexity is equally present in the fragment because it is not a problem of scales. So, to address the liquid world and its inherent risks, the first task is, according to Morin, to contextualize. Things only make sense if seen in context, like a word in a sentence or a human action within a human culture. When looking at humans in our world, we see both unity and diversity, a surprising genetic, physiological, and emotional unity: we all smile and cry and experience pain and joy, but this similarity translates into a great diversity of cultures and behaviors. Within the framework of the globalized world, Morin proposes:

We have to recognize others as different and equal to us. If we see others as entirely different, we cannot understand them. We cannot see what makes them original and different if we see them as completely identical.

As is already common in complexity, this new paradox gives us a clue to approach liquid risks through more flexible references and from their own contexts, not isolated from reality or with prejudices of differentiation or equality. These are globalized times in which complexity and technological acceleration no longer have scale because they cannot be measured.

The digital showcase

The size of the digital network we are immersed in today is virtually infinite. At this moment, hundreds of millions of mobile phones, computers, tablets, and even refrigerators are connected to each other, producing and receiving data of the most varied nature and generating information that, in turn, feeds back and makes the world more "intelligent." We would say that it is a network of incalculable complexity. Every second we spend connected to this web of billions of nodes, our ideas, data, transactions, and decisions are recorded forever, eliminating virtually all privacy. There is, therefore, no way to live on this planet without being under the potential scrutiny of whoever wants to follow in our footsteps. There is no doubt that anonymity is becoming a highly valued asset for many. Life under this level of exposure is not easy. The possibility of tracking our movements in detail makes many people uncomfortable. It is a kind of window open to the street that we do not control, and through it, we give third parties the right to look carefully inside. As an example, just review the usage contracts of some free applications. These record and transmit information about places, purchases, and even the vital signs of those who use them, with the purpose of feeding information systems that end up knowing more about us than we can imagine. Just out of curiosity, review the data provided when you wear a smartwatch, and you will understand the amount of privacy you are sharing.

The price we pay for being part of this global digital community is the amount of data we give up. Not being fully aware of this makes us highly vulnerable, and security still seems not to recognize that this new and complex reality imposes a challenge of proportions not estimated until today. Because we do not know them, it is not easy to determine the magnitude of the risks hidden behind big data and, even less so, the implications derived from its analysis. Additionally, understanding the nature of these risks requires such specialized knowledge that very few will be able to identify hidden threats.

The expansion rate of the capabilities of information systems based on data correlation is astonishing. We lack the filters to protect ourselves from the algorithms that model us, predicting consumer trends, travel sites, the time we spend using our mobile phones, or the hours we travel. We have become an open book for these algorithms. On the other hand, it is so attractive and easy to consume the offer presented to us that we succumb to the temptation and even become addicted to transferring data. We want the most innovative cell phone and the most recently launched smartwatch, and we dream of an electric vehicle that will take us on autopilot with minimal effort from one place to another. Increasingly, smart technology is fed by our perception that doing less is a metaphor for a lavish lifestyle.

As humans, we are prone to be subjective when estimating risks when we are involved with the environment or believe we know it well. Hence, our over-dependence on the digital world imitates our ability to assess the magnitude and power of threats. The freedom of engaging with the digital is so powerful that it can easily enthrall those who live hyperconnected in its multiple dimensions. This, in turn, reduces the levels of defense against the risks coming out of the digital realm. For now, and until we develop sufficient defenses, the recommendation is to become aware that we live in a digital showcase and that, like Hansel and Gretel, we leave footprints wherever we go.

9

Multiplexed in a nudist beach

Every idea extended to infinity,
it becomes its own opposite.

-Georg Wilhelm Friedrich Hegel

The accelerated changes in the current pace of life and the uncertainty they cause are not just a passing phase. They are shaping our society and our future. They lead us to ask ourselves if we are prepared for the liquid risks we are now facing and those we will face in the future. When I refer to the future, I am not imagining a time that is far away but rather what will happen to us in the very short term. It is a moment when we are obliged to understand what is going on around us if we intend to address it successfully.

Forecasting is not just a challenge but a crucial skill for professionals in our times. It is essential to create a vision, even with thick lines, of the future and assign some probability value to each one of the scenarios of tomorrow. Without them, we navigate blindly in the ocean of change. We cannot approach the future believing that tomorrow will be the same as today. The unexpected arrival of COVID-19 was evidence of this statement.

When forecasting, it is worth noting that, as soon as we begin to scratch the surface of the problem, in this process of accelerated changes, the solutions will arrive with delay compared to the issues. However, careful examination is essential to determine whether a pattern emerges or if, on the contrary, we are facing a succession of chaotic and unconnected events. In this sense, let us begin by characterizing our present-time reality. If we do it, we will realize that with the acceleration of technology, the barrier between the virtual and the real gets broken, releasing us from the physical constraints. As I will explain in the following paragraphs, individuals turn into *multiplexed* beings, living in a liquid world of infinite possibilities. Multiplexing is a term borrowed from electronics. It refers to using a single channel to simultaneously send multiple signals. This is possible because, through multiplexing, signals can be segmented in time, passed forward in small packets at high speed through the same medium, and then recovered and restored at the destination. Multiplexed beings do something similar: They are able to fragment their time into small packages and simultaneously focus their attention on the merge of the real and virtual in an accelerated frenzy in which they pay attention to everything and nothing at the same time. *Multiplexing is the only way to vibrate at the same frequency as the liquid world.* Thus, if in the recent past, there were eight or ten university programs amongst which we had to choose to shape our professional career, now there are multiple paths, many of them circumventing a college or a university, to design and build up a career. Similarly, if, in the past, your lifespan only allowed you to have a limited number of friends and relationships, with digital social networks, you can have thousands or millions of followers (certainly not friends) with whom you can engage. Where there was a television channel with a set of rigid schedules of contents, there is now a door to infinite channels with a wide range of topics. This process of building complexity has reached such an extreme that you can even choose from a variety of sexual genders without being constrained to simply being a man or a woman.

Multiplexed beings, although they carry an endless number of possibilities, are also carriers of a number of vulnerabilities. For each one, innumerable actors may be willing to exploit the exposed flanks. Thus, if we are careless, the world of infinite possibilities can be turned into a world of infinite risks. Multiplexed beings move between real and virtual worlds without stopping at their borders because they do not care about either one of them. Their minds have integrated the transition between both worlds, allowing them to smoothly move between them. It is, in some way, a universe with new space-time references. They are global individuals who are everywhere and nowhere. Although they do not intend to detach themselves from the physical dimension that ties them to the local, they no longer belong to a place. They would rather belong to a world of infinite places. However, this ubiquity carries an omnipresent risk. What gives us maximum freedom of movement is, at the same time, the most sophisticated remote observation and control system. Infinite possibilities exist because technology, increasingly powerful, portable, and easy, allows it. We have a cell phone that is never more than a meter away from our bodies, and it never (it should never) interrupt the connection to a global network, marking our geographical position, recording communications, and storing practically all our everyday activities. From how many steps we take to the hours we spend asleep and those we spend awake. As if that were not enough, we connect to social networks to share thoughts, ideas, projects, opinions, and moods. In addition, we broadcast live about what happens in our surroundings.

The techno-panopticon

The way we willingly disclose our private lives entirely has a meandric but not far relationship to the concept of the panopticon, a model prison developed by the British philosopher and jurist Jeremy Bentham in the 18th century. Bentham conceived of a building where prisoners would be constantly watched by a guard located in a central tower. The prison's architectural layout was designed to allow the guards in the center to see all the prisoners simultaneously. In contrast, the prisoners would not be able to see the guards. This creates a situation where prisoners do not know when they are being observed and behave as if they are constantly being watched. The panopticon would lead prisoners to self-monitor and discipline themselves. The fear of constant observation and imminent punishment would become a habit, enabling the normalization and discipline of individuals within the prison system. Foucault used the panopticon concept to illustrate how disciplinary power can operate in other social institutions like schools, hospitals, and factories. The idea of the panopticon was relevant to critical theory and the understanding of surveillance, control, and discipline in contemporary society. Unfortunately, Foucault, who died in 1984, did not have the opportunity to witness how, in postmodern culture, the panopticon evolved and adapted to new forms of surveillance and social control. While the original architectural version of the panopticon has become less common today, the idea of constant surveillance and disciplinary control remains a central feature in our world.

Technology has enabled new forms of surveillance and social control that are more subtle and omnipresent than the disciplinary techniques of the past. Security cameras, facial recognition, online monitoring, and social media are some of the expanded surveillance and control methods. Thus, in postmodern society, discipline is internalized through self-surveillance and self-discipline, meaning individuals control themselves to adapt to society's norms and expectations. Evidence of this is the way individuals present their lives on social media. The "watching entity" has given way to a mode of digital showcase, where displaying oneself on networks becomes a prophylactic and addictive validation of ourselves.

Recently, South Korean philosopher Byung-Chul Han has argued that the disciplinary society has given way to the *Performance Society*. According to Han, the disciplinary society, as described by Michel Foucault, was based on repression and prohibition, where discipline was imposed from above and exercised through constant surveillance, normalization, and individualized correction. In contrast, the performance society is characterized by excess positivity and self-exploitation. To a large extent, individuals voluntarily submit to discipline and control rather than having it imposed from the outside. Discipline and surveillance are no longer seen as external restrictions but as means to achieve personal success and satisfaction. In the performance society, everything becomes a task, including happiness. Life is seen as an ongoing project. Individuals must be productive and efficient in everything they do, even in their free time, constantly improving and optimizing their performance. If we understand Han, the new panopticon has been internalized within each of us, and it is no longer necessary to be watched from the outside because voluntarily, through our smartphones, we broadcast our lives, live and unfiltered, making public what was once private. This behavior is not an addition to the postmodern way of living; it is intrinsic to society — showing ourselves is part of our self-exploitation, making us feel more productive within the performance society. We have reached a paradoxical point for security. Under these new forms of surveillance, self-monitoring makes us feel more accepted and productive in society. That is why it should not surprise us that many telecommunications and technology companies have already decided to "give away" their best phones and other gadgets for free because we have voluntarily and addictively agreed to carry our own moveable *techno-panopticon*.

In this new world, disclosing our private lives is no longer considered a threat (although it is) but a dangerous temptation. Social networks have become a means of recognizing and validating anyone's life. Recording and posting every sort of content online are antidotes to exclusion. An outcome of all this is that the boundaries between the public and the private have been diluted, so delving deep into the lives of others has become a piece of cake. This dimension where the dividing walls are translucent, and people enjoy showing off—is just a different and introspective form of the mentioned digital showcase.

Paradoxically, the endless options that blur the public from the private build infinite opportunities for anonymity. The culture of the avatar multiplexes the individual and transforms her into anything she desires. Curiously, with these borders blurred and merged, the private realm becomes infinite, and everyone feels they have the right to give their opinion and make decisions about everyone else. Ultra-exposure minimizes the reputational paradigm. Everything can be brought to maximum public scrutiny, and no one is exempt from criticism and questioning. Social networks are, for these purposes, the indelible record of the community. Can we then aspire to security in a world of infinite possibilities? We should say that multiplexed life is not antagonistic to security. Although the decision to open the private sphere to the world raises a significant vulnerability, everything will depend on how you do it and who accompanies you. Even if the threat is still there, the reward is worth it. The issue here is that the only way for a multiplexed being to live in a world of infinite possibilities is to assume the risk of digital nudity since the alternative (for some) would be the unbearable parochial and constrained three-dimensional reality of the physical. This practice of lowering the costs of risk by massifying vulnerabilities is similar to the legalization of drugs. It is based on the false belief that by regulating its sale, it stops being dangerous and harms the health of those who consume it. Ultimately, all responsibility is transferred to the individual who, tempted by infinite possibilities, could feel invulnerable, thus losing his consciousness in the face of risk, devoured by the ultra-exposure mentioned above to both the real and the virtual.

Therefore, the great challenge of protection transcends the mere physical plane, in which electronic systems are managed or the protection personnel are supervised. Its function must point to the first security commandment: creating risk awareness. In this world of infinite possibilities, the security professional cannot remain subject to his own space since he is called to transcend equally and to develop a—multiplexed—strategy of "evangelization" if he intends to create such consciousness. Therefore, the function of security will have to evolve from a debate revolving around resilience to becoming a driving factor of a profound change in human beings and their way of relating to the world. If, at some point, security was conceived, within a spatial metaphor, as a model of layers (rings) of protection, placing the individual as a fragile object in the center of a space with well-defined edges, the current paradigm is its complete opposite. It conceives of the multiplexed human being as a creator of security halos built from individual risk awareness and aimed at protecting multiple dimensions. This new model is not based on risk mitigation but on minimizing potentially risky realities. In simpler terms, if human beings can create an infinite number of realms (virtual and real) between which they move smoothly, they will then have to develop environments of minimal risks but where individuals will have full awareness of the risks that are run in the process. Returning to the nudist beach metaphor, everyone who takes their clothes off in this space will get a sense of liberty because nothing comes between them and the environment. Still, they will be fully aware that they are living at the point of greatest vulnerability. It is that sort of mindfulness, where you experience the omnipresence of risk, that will protect you in this new liquid world.

The security of the physical plane, so often associated with the value of trust, is forced in its evolution to assume that only through awareness of risk can it offer some guarantee and, in turn, validate itself to access the world of infinite possibilities. This security, with full risk awareness, is itself a kind of security.

Security will no longer be a process that reduces the vulnerabilities of an object or an environment. Still, building full awareness turns the subject into an axis and active evaluator of the dangers surrounding them. This allows her to decide on a path to deconstruct these risks, even before they become evident. It is not about building a pre-crime unit, like the one imagined in the film *Minority Report*, capable of stopping crime before it is committed. For now, we only manage to predict the future very clumsily, although we have powerful AI tools. In the technology-enabled world of infinite possibilities, security will increasingly depend on the reasonable judgment of multiplexed and global human beings.

Securization: the end of the road for public space

I use this neologism to designate a phenomenon that is beginning to mark the developed societies of the planet. It refers to the proliferation of private spaces within public spaces, producing a distancing effect between citizens that, when it reaches a limit, ends up diluting the social ties between people. This concept inspired me when I was reading *Ground Control*, a book written by Anne Minton, a British journalist. There, she posed the idea of the privatization of public spaces. Although Minton does not use *securization* to describe the phenomenon, in the disciplines of Urban Studies and Sociology, securization describes the trend where private spaces and security concerns impact the organization of urban spaces. It involves the prioritization of security over public access, potentially leading to the privatization of public spaces. In her book, Minton argues that privatizing public spaces does not necessarily enhance security. Nonetheless, my perspective diverges: transforming public or private spaces into zones where individuals connect to wireless networks and engage in smartphone conversations rather than interacting with others in the physical space, to some extent, liquefy human relationships.

Securization may seem contradictory or inapplicable in Latin America since, in this region, the codes that regulate interpersonal relationships are practically nonexistent. In addition, people there have a very close personal distance, which means that interaction at much smaller distances is considered socially permissible, and this is different from what happens in other parts of the West. However, even in the cities of this region, the phenomenon is more present than we are aware. An example of what I call securization is the proliferation of large commercial spaces in closed and artificially climatized buildings. These buildings work as public spaces of contemplation that can only be seen but not used. This is the case of beautiful gardens cared for in detail, encapsulated in glass bubbles or green areas that cannot be touched. This transformation of physical space into an area of visual enjoyment is one more aspect of the virtualization of reality, in which the tangible becomes a landscape. This distancing through securitization is another paradox of the liquid world. The more connections we create in virtuality, reaching the point of becoming multiplexed beings, the more we distance human relationships in physical space. The public space should also be the agora, where the social fabric is strengthened, and the space for developing a citizenry is more aligned with its everyday reality. The problem is that when it is limited or privatized, its effect is projected on people, isolating them even more than insecurity and the pandemic have already done. However, security has a second, utterly liquid effect, making people believe that it is never enough, perhaps more challenging to observe, although it dramatically impacts people. Along with the privatization of public space, the citizens generate a feeling of false security since it is assumed that one can be safer in controlled or closed spaces. It is a kind of agoraphobia or anxiety about a non-existent insecurity. Still, it is induced by people's exacerbated control over their environment through hyperconnectivity to networks.

It is now common to realize how people avoid going to places where the quality of the mobile phone signal is poor or non-existent. We have reached such a high level of dependency (or addiction) to control systems that we are terrified of being outside the coverage area of mobile networks. We are unaware that public roads are potentially more risky. However, they are subject to the social control of the citizen, who can detect, deter, and even stop, in some cases, criminal action. On the other hand, the police, in their work of prevention and custody of open spaces, are obliged to generate trust and respect, which usually does not happen in closed spaces protected by private security. Cities are large social laboratories that demand permanent attention to maintain their fragile balance of coexistence. Modifying public spaces or converting public spaces into areas of mere contemplation, in which citizens are not allowed to engage, can lead to insecurity. I have seen many beautiful cities, but without people to enjoy them. They are like display cases or dioramas in a museum instead of spaces for civic engagement. Securization is not a liquid risk linked directly to power but to the ability to exercise social control, which in essence is a sophisticated way of dominating the other without force, but rather something much more powerful, dependency.

...if we are waiting for more stable times to develop new projects, we have to understand that complexity pervades all our endeavors.

10

Productivity is now nomadic

The allure of the distant and the difficult is deceptive.
The great opportunity is where you are.

-John Burroughs

We used to believe that one of the conditions of growth was the stability of the environment and that it was impossible to lay the foundations of a strong, long-lasting structure in turbulent realities or imbalanced systems. Such a belief has lost most of its significance in the liquid world. Uncertainty and unpredictability support the development of new models adapted to growth dynamics amid turbulence. This is because, looking to the future, there are no signs that reality is moving towards areas of stability and certainty. Then, if we are waiting for more stable times to develop new projects, we have to understand that complexity pervades all our endeavors. Indeed, those who understand the inherent complexity of the times we are living in have an increasing competitive advantage over those who are waiting for calmer terrain to further their projects. I have a friend who is a mathematical genius. His work is based on identifying correlations between real-world events and the variations of the hundreds of stock indices in the world's financial markets. These correlations are encoded on high-speed servers that run algorithms to buy and sell stocks, futures, currencies, and anything listed on the stock exchanges in milliseconds. The higher the variations, the higher will be the profits obtained. His model is built on the accelerated volatility of a reality fueled by uncertainty.

For some time now, the large financial movements of the liquid world have no longer depended on the solidity of the economic results of companies but on the infinite possibilities of complexity. At a press conference at Euro 2020 (played in 2021 after the effects of the pandemic), Cristiano Ronaldo, a famous forward, and striker of the Portuguese national team and soccer superstar, moved away two bottles of Coca-Cola that were on the table. That gesture was interpreted to mean that people should drink water instead of soda. That same day, the soft drink company's shares fell 1.6% on the NYSE, about four billion dollars. It is not unreasonable to assume that the drop in the company's share price had to do with Ronaldo's snub. In any case, the key is that it is difficult to estimate cause-and-effect relationships in complex environments. Therefore, predicting that a couple of soda bottles placed for marketing could end up having the opposite effect is almost impossible.

In 1983, Michel Foucault wrote the Preface to Anti-Oedipus, Capitalism and Schizophrenia, a book by Gilles Deleuze and Félix Guattari, where humans are analyzed as part of the social machine and the capitalist means of production. In his preface, Foucault outlines the transformation process towards a world that no longer conforms to reality but opts instead for the possibilities of virtuality. "The multiple should be preferred to the unitary, differentiation to unity, mobile arrangements to systems." What is productive is no longer sedentary but nomadic, Foucault states. In some way, Deleuze and Guattari sustain that only by connecting to a flow can the individual get integrated into the great production machine in the current world. Perhaps in 1983, it was still difficult to understand the dynamics of globalization enhanced by technological development, but the microchip era was already advancing and beginning to accelerate our world. Something similar to what happened to the Soviet Union, which, having the largest intelligence apparatus of its time, was unable to see the coming transformation towards the liquid world (which caused its large production machines to remain disconnected from reality), can happen to all those who do not understand that a new and mobile organization, which flows at the pace of accelerated times, will be an ideal tool to avoid succumbing to complexity. All of this leads us to reflect on the model for the security of organizations and even nations if, in addition to liquid threats, one has to act and make all sorts of decisions within a complex, volatile, and challenging environment.

When I referred to security in the world of infinite possibilities, I explained the need to close the gaps in digital vulnerabilities and transform the individual into a subject (that is, an actor with agency) from which it is possible to generate security instead of conceiving and conceptualizing the individual as if it were an object without criteria or consciousness. In this case, organizational models, no matter how dynamic or liquid they may be, require some structure to operate. The objective is to optimize the use of resources in the functions that add more value in visualization, awareness creation, analysis, prevention, and risk mitigation. It is about breaking down security into processes that, on the one hand, can be automated to the maximum and consume minimal human resources, and on the other, allow risk scenarios to be determined and prevented using the capabilities and experience of professionals trained for such purposes.

Automation taken to the extreme is in itself another liquid risk since what is automated is interconnected to a world that now has infinite possibilities and opens new vulnerabilities for sabotage, interruptions, and cyber-attacks to occur on critical infrastructures and services. We have reached a time of unstable realities, and it seems that these have come to settle, making uncertainty the common constant. Although the infinite of the possible can always be superimposed on reality, in security, we have to assume both levels: the emergence of the here and now and the opportunities for continuous change.

From individual freedom to the petty tyrant

I am persuaded that nomadic complexity is accompanied by another process, perhaps more profound, already described by Ulrich Beck in Reflexive Modernization: Politics, Tradition, and Aesthetics. I am referring to the individualization of the human being. With the arrival of reflexive modernity, new ways have emerged that have replaced the old schemes of the industrialized world. Rising as a force aiming at introducing a balance to the anonymity brought to us by mass society, an accelerated individualization of human beings has occurred. One of its many consequences is that individuals no longer require representation to access power or depend on large corporate structures to exercise their profession or trade. Globalization and the accelerated development of information technologies have turned knowledge into a public asset, much more valuable than those held by any brick-and-mortar company. What I am trying to convey is that people have shed the labels and uniformities of the masses to become individuals integrated into a complex, technologically accelerated network of flows and connections in which they live, work and have fun without the need to mediate with structures that limit their options, as they did in industrial society. The old belief that to get into the system, you had to ascend the social ladder has expired and has given way to a world of infinite possibilities. The dynamics of the liquid world accelerated even further after the COVID-19 pandemic, bringing a paradigm shift in how people live and work. Faced with the massive loss of jobs in thousands of companies due to the abrupt decline in the economy of some sectors and the imposition of restrictive measures for mobility, the digitalization of production modes experienced a dizzying rise riding on a process already in development.

The parallel processes of horizontalization and fragmentation of organizations have given individuals new possibilities to earn a living in freer and more independent formats. Proof of this is that, during the months following the pandemic's end, many mass consumption or service companies faced difficulty filling jobs at the lowest levels of the chains. Although it was argued that the reason for this was the financial aid governments provided to the population, many realized that remote work made employees feel freer and gave them a better income compared to minimum wage jobs and long working hours.

Freedom is implicit in the posited individualization of society. The men and women of the liquid society are no longer obliged to be part of a hierarchical corporate structure or join a career in public administration to climb positions. The infinite possibilities digital technology has opened allow individuals to connect to hundreds of networks to reach the market of services and products that flow through the web.

The digital economy also operates in a multiplexed world without borders between the real and the virtual. It is a metaverse of infinite possibilities in which you can navigate along various flows and make enough income for an independent life. This means that, simultaneously, you can be a driver for Uber or Doordash, produce and monetize content on Instagram, and create NFTs while deciding what part of the savings can be allocated to investments in the stock market using applications like Robinhood. However, not everything is as good as it seems, and individualization can become a substitute rather than a path to freedom. Only in countries with a certain level of development and civil liberties are new paradigms of individualization being created and flourishing. In contrast, nations with authoritarian regimes take advantage of digital technology to control their population at an extreme level. Individualization does not give rise to individual freedom but to the dissolution of the social fabric, breaking the links that glue together the movements of demand and change in those societies. As expected, the authoritarian response to the process of individualization of society is not only limited to the large structures of the States. Being a network model, it is straightforward to replicate it in multiple directions, that becomes the new liquid threat of creating tiny tyrants in civil organizations, in which positions are imposed and polarized. This common practice in political parties, neighborhood communities, or professional unions often extends to corporations, institutions, and cultural and academic spheres.

The guarantee of freedom of association, which in the past had been a strength of democracies due to its open nature, has become its main vulnerability to the authoritarianism exercised by petty tyrants. To prevent this, it is necessary to strengthen cultures and identities. Since individualization is an unstoppable process, societies and organizations need to generate a sense of belonging among their members. It is a new dynamic balance in the social fabric. As reflective actors (since they would express this new modernity), individuals would not have to respond to dogmas or ideologies to be part of a community. Still, they would voluntarily accept and internalize purposes that make them converge in the same flow of interests. In mobile arrangements, nothing remains calm for long. The world is now a torrent of forces and counterforces that will never be balanced. Globalization and the fractalization of tyrannies oppose individualization and the freedom to produce. They are each, in some way, the liquid synthesis of the times because, despite their antagonisms, neither can paralyze the other; they only compete to stay ahead.

What was once solid and almost immovable as truth is now liquid and unpredictable, creating a sense of uncertainty and unpredictability in the modern media landscape.

11

The blood that feeds the system

*In times of universal deception,
telling the truth is a revolutionary act.*

-George Orwell

Never before have narratives been so present in the vocabulary of the people. It is no longer just politicians and marketing strategists who brand their narratives like swords in combat. Instead, the concept has become another realm of the liquid world where multiple battles are fought. In the liquid context, narrative refers to a persuasive tale that aims to tell the story in a way that is convenient for political, ideological, commercial, or other purposes. The goal of a narrative is not just to align followers but to turn them into activists for a cause, thereby shaping public opinion. Currently, the accelerated expansion of communications and the unlimited access to the internet has facilitated traction for narratives that seek to establish organized visions of reality through the leading social media platforms. This liquid power of narratives is not new, and its origin dates back to the era of large media monopolies. With the arrival of cable television in the early 1980s, 24-hour news channels such as CNN (1980) and Fox (1996) realized that to maintain viewers' attention, they had to turn everyday events into stories. Those were the times of never-ending sequences of stories, chained one to the other. In this way, those narratives would build a plot to shape (guide) public opinion according to the conveniences and interests of political or economic interest groups. Very soon, the newscasts and the news ceased to be a catalog of independent events told one after another to become a collection of stories intertwined in a chronological sequence that had to be told like a novel in chapters. The anchors of news narration became storytellers with great skills for interviewing and research, and as expected in this context, politics, as raw material for news, got a stellar space.

The political-narrative binomial is natural because they belong to each other. What is interesting is that now, the narrative dimension is equally inherent to the strategies, whether for leaders to ascend the scales of power or to build a brand with millions of fans through Instagram. It is important to note that the narrative space has become embedded in a world of infinite possibilities. One of the consequences of which is that, in the stories that are told, it matters little whether or not they are fiction, nonfiction or truthful. What has value is being part of a story to achieve a goal. It is there where narratives become liquid because the facts are no longer the axis of the story, and this has blurred their materiality and become risky. The narrative is the blood that flows through the networks. It carries and brings everything in a permanent flow that keeps the system alive. With it, and through it, reality and possibility can be exchanged as in a room of mirrors where, by reflecting each other, the real dissolves to be rewritten in the alternative, according to convenience and in alignment with the interests of the storyteller. What was once solid and almost immovable as truth is now liquid and unpredictable, creating a sense of uncertainty and unpredictability in the modern media landscape. In this logic, we can only hope to tangentially approach the moving contours of the facts since we no longer know if they are materializations of reality or constructs in virtuality. As in the Maltese Falcon, in this new liquid world, anything could unexpectedly and suddenly turn into this *stuff that dreams are made of.*

The fusion of narratives with the acceleration of the complex has transformed truth into quantum facts that, as in physics, only have a probability value of materializing in reality. A kind of Heisenberg Uncertainty Principle of history, where there is never simultaneous certainty of the level at which it is told and how the events occur. Each social network is a channel to tell something. What are you thinking? What's going on? What are you doing? These are the questions that networks ask to motivate their users to tell stories; it doesn't matter which one, if it is real, fictitious, or to whom it belongs. What matters is being there, connected to the narrative flow, in the happening of the timeline, where the truth goes viral or is devalued according to whatever the audience likes or decides. Now, as much as multiplexed beings live in that diffuse zone between reality and possibility, in the liquid world, events occur that cannot be dissolved by narratives. However, there is always a way to interpret them and make them seem favorable to the interests of whoever has the power to change them.

At the end of the 20th century, spin doctors appeared on the global stage. They were specialists in manipulating stories aiming at doing damage control. All the presidents of the United States, from Nixon to Joe Biden, have had their own spin doctors. They became indispensable figures of political and strategic communication. They were called to put out fires whenever those in power realized it was impossible to change reality. We cannot be naive by believing that reality is not lied to or accommodated from the political stands. This has always been the case. What is different now is that, since those wielding power promote the liquid narratives, not only is reality twisted to fit it with the leader's storytelling, but a world of possibilities is created where the official version is shaped to

105

seem coherent to the activists who consume the stories. It is a kind of dissociation from reality where there is a parallel world where all the elements fit perfectly as if they were puzzle pieces. As if indifferent to this dynamic, at the level of reality, the facts, behaving as endowed with free will, do not always allow complete or logically coherent stories to be told.

If, at any point in history, the phrase that defines *politics as the art of the possible* can be more accurate, it is now. With liquid narratives, it is no longer necessary to construct the objective conditions for change because, in the flow of infinite possibilities, the reality is like a mobile stage assembled and disassembled to be adjusted to the expectations and interests of the leader. As French writer Christian Salmon points out in his book *The Age of Confrontation*, "*Communicators have replaced action with the story, deliberation with distraction, statecraft with stagecraft.*"

Robert J. Shiller, professor of economics at Yale University and winner of the 2013 Nobel Prize in Economics, wrote a book called *Narrative Economics: How narratives go viral and generate great economic events*. According to Shiller, the stories we tell ourselves impact our reality and can sometimes generate major crises. Some narratives are timeless and are recycled based on events that emerge from reality. This has happened with topics such as fear and hope around technology and the need to recover moral rectitude. Hence, there are developments or stories about the feelings of certain groups that influence the economy, whether unions are corrupt or the rich are evil. Although it may not seem like it, liquid narratives are one of security's most critical challenges. Their ability to dissolve truth and reality puts in trouble both public order and justice. If everything is relativized, the rule of law loses its references and leaves no soil to find its roots. Without laws, the justice system is meaningless, and the border between citizen certainty and the gray area of crime will become increasingly blurred.

By not having a defined category, the parts of a heterarchical system can be ordered according to their purposes.

12

The kingdom of the heterarchical

According to what we have said in this book, an organization will be liquid if it has a unique ability to adapt to environmental changes. Like water or any other fluid that takes the shape of a container, the quality of something being liquid differs from that of being resilient, which is the property of being flexible when dealing with adversity. A resilient organization temporarily changes its shape to absorb the impact of what affects it. It returns to its natural state after absorbing the experience and sometimes learning from it. It's like bamboo when it waves in the wind. The liquid organization does not have pre-established rules; it adapts to circumstances and follows the path of least resistance to achieve its objectives. It is capable of deforming and adapting multiple times if the environment demands it. There are no criteria for efficiency or profit maximization; the only important thing is to achieve the objectives.

Organized crime is an excellent example of a liquid organization. Although, at times, its acts may be motivated by power, it will do what it needs, at whatever cost it believes is necessary, and without legal or ethical restrictions, to increase its earnings or maintain its position. Organized crime operates according to a model of closely intertwined networks, a practice that confers the possibility of using infinite alternative routes in case of difficulties. Although organized crime has existed for a long time, globalization and technological acceleration have multiplied its modes of operation and its interconnection possibilities. The pace of change and successive adaptation is natural to liquid organizations, hence their significant advantage over the rest of the world. It is an advantage that opens a gap separating those who reconfigure themselves under the pressures of changing reality and those who cannot see change coming or are so rigid that they cannot adapt to the increasing speed of change.

Although not all organized crime is liquid, it is getting increasingly liquid for survival reasons. In the recent past, it was common for this crime to be organized according to a hierarchical pyramidal system, in which a prominent figure at the top, in the style of Pablo Escobar and the Medellín cartel, exercised ironclad control. Although Escobar managed terrorism and hitman networks, after he died in 1993, the drug business in Colombia was reorganized into a complex system of paramilitary and guerrilla groups with much more liquid characteristics. Mexican cartels such as *Jalisco Nueva Generación* and *Sinaloa* have diversified into multi-dimensional structures through which dozens of illicit businesses operate on several continents. In the latter's case, it overcame the capture and extradition of its leader, Joaquín "El Chapo" Guzmán Loera, without major operational disruptions. It is known that the Sinaloa cartel has groups of financial experts on its payroll who are responsible for the detailed management of the organization's funds, from investing in farmland to money laundering through the purchase of properties. In the same way, logistics chains transport drugs by different means to the United States, Europe, and Australia. They even have small cargo submarines that submerge in the waters of the Pacific from Mexico to California.

However, not all liquid organizations are criminal. Some transnational companies observe and learn quickly from the liquid world. Although they must operate in regulated environments, make profits, and operate according to strict ethical codes, they have crossed the gap of accelerated readaptation and far surpass traditional business models. For example, Uber, the passenger transportation company, is practically liquid. It adapts to almost every country where it decides to operate, meeting the universal need of moving people, objects, and food from one place to another, using a network of independent drivers and vehicles to do so. The company has the most cars in the world, and it does not own any. Amazon, Google, Airbnb, Netflix, and Apple are also examples of innovation in the face of the challenges of the fluid and complex dynamics of globalization.

A more approximate definition of a liquid organization can be attempted by resorting to the concept of antifragility and calling them *antifragile organizations*. Antifragility is a neologism coined by the Lebanese-born mathematician Nassim Nicholas Taleb to describe that which is adaptable, resilient, and takes advantage of chaos and uncertainty to grow and succeed. Perhaps liquid does not have all these properties. We can probably only say that it is capable of surviving vicissitudes, although the fundamental difference between this and Taleb's concept of antifragility is that in the latter, environmental factors perceived as threats improve the system, not only to adapt it but to make it fitter in the face of adversity. This reminds us of Charles Darwin's concept of natural selection leading to the survival of the fittest. The difference is that liquid organizations do not want or need to improve. They exist to accomplish their goals. If they do not work, they disappear or transform themselves to adapt. In this latter case, they will go over the path of least resistance to achieve their goals. This is why criminal organizations do not seek to be shapers or creators of reality. They would instead go *stealth*, merging with the landscape. If their leaders are public figures and become well known, this constitutes a defense mechanism aimed at protecting those who work at lower hierarchical levels, closer to the operations, generally in complete anonymity.

The liquid organization is an expression of postmodernity. It is how Zygmunt Bauman defined our contemporary world, calling it liquid modernity:

"In the volatile world of liquid modernity, where almost no form remains unchanged long enough to get and ensure long-term reliability, walking is better than sitting, running is better than walking, and surfing is better than running."

Thus, reality, immersed in constant change, devalues itself and gives way to a new reality that will be devalued one more time. In this dynamic, survival can only be achieved if some rules or procedures are ignored. In this sense, it is practically impossible for the institutional and formal democracies of the Western world to become liquid since their strengths lie in the rigidity of their foundations and the solid establishment of values, customs, and traditions. Thus, the liquid world slips with imperceptible ease through the vulnerabilities of States with all the advantages that uncontrolled power provides.

Some countries have understood that in liquid times, representative democracies worldwide are under tremendous pressure to resist the flattening of power structures leveraged by communication technologies that erase the borders of space and time and the amplification power of social networks. Therefore, relationships between individuals are more like heterarchical networks with multiple interconnection nodes and channels of participation and influence in society's public life. But these capacities to involve more actors in the collective decision-making are also impacted by liquid organizations dedicated to bending the will of the majority and, from their anonymity, intervening in electoral processes, even before citizens have been able to decide which option they are going to support with both their voice and votes. To this must be added the automation of voting systems, which, instead of providing transparency to the democratic exercise, make it more complex and, therefore, easier to be imperceptibly intervened to favor those who have the power to manipulate it. Faced with such circumstances, those corrupt governments delegitimized by abusive practices of power *liquefy*, like criminal organizations, to maintain their advantages and privileges. The natural and historical convergence between dictators and criminal networks has found a multidimensional space to flourish in liquid dynamics, leaving justice far behind in its attempt to stop and dismantle them. The political-criminal synergy is more than the sum of its parts. Regimes acquire criminal skills in their transnational networks, which, in turn, obtain a niche from which to establish their operations, thus deploying their criminal potential safely. Faced with this phenomenon, democratic governments and international justice have a diminished capacity to respond, and only when this combination begins to threaten regional stability are measures taken, mainly of an economic nature, to block or undermine the sources of financing. However, given the liquid nature of convergences, they quickly adapt to new conditions and mutate, both in their forms and functions, to guarantee survival. At this point of the juxtaposition of political and criminal planes, liquid risks arise, being difficult to contain and even more difficult to mitigate.

The political-criminal overlap gives rise to criminal States, new forms of populism, denatured armed forces placed at the service of tyrannies, and large propaganda apparatuses. Likewise, this overlap houses sophisticated systems of repression and social domination and spaces for the trafficking of everything illegal that may exist on the planet. All are risks of criminal political origin but are now liquid due to the complexity of the environment, the dynamics of organizations, and the slowness of democratic institutions that should mitigate or neutralize them. However, this power that allows organizations to become liquid is not without costs. In the transformation, other risks also arise since, as hierarchies dissolve, power must be exercised under new paradigms, and relations of subordination mutate to the new geometry of networks, where the categories to classify objects, individuals, societies, systems, or ideologies have stopped being static.

Binary classifications are losing their meaning and ability to sort things out. Thus, it is not worth dividing politics between left or right; gender is no longer just male or female, and even national States now respond to a wide variety of interests and do not behave as monolithic blocks. We are now entering a multiplexed space of reality. We could call this new stage the era of heterarchies. *Heterarchy refers to a new way of ordering the world, in which the relationships between people, organizations, or societies can be classified in multiple ways, prioritizing in these classifications the most flexible structures, made up of networks, instead of the classic hierarchical pyramids.* Heterarchy divides or unites according to interests, tends to be polyvalent, and to a certain extent undifferentiated when it does not respond to a specific classification. In heterarchical systems, elements have the potential to be classified in different ways, and each one is interwoven horizontally in a network with its peers. By not having a defined category, the parts of a heterarchical system can be ordered according to their purposes. Therefore, an element can ally against a particular objective and an adversary against another. The heterarchical order is an undifferentiated and non-hierarchical kingdom that takes shape and aligns according to a unity of purpose, in which, once its objective is achieved, it merges into its network to adjust again according to new interests or purposes.

The planet faces a new organizational paradigm that challenges the fundamental notion of the identity principle on which Western philosophy is based, A = A. Faced with this, any previous reference has been contradictory since then; something can be different from itself and be classified according to its changing interest or purpose. The heterarchical order is about that new way of arranging the world. Faced with this panorama, the time has come for these forces, until now undifferentiated, to disclose themselves, perhaps because they are aligned in their purposes or because they feel threatened by counterforces that try to oppose them. In any case, they seem to have the advantage and are determined to advance on multiple levels and agendas.

The critical issue is *the antifragility of the heterarchical order* since this is in itself a powerful system of inhibition for those who seek to change or dismantle it through the traditional or institutional means of the recent past. This being the case, the challenge before us is of significant proportions. Therefore, it is necessary to become aware of these processes and, secondly, to learn to identify the flows and connections in this multidimensional board of blurred lines on which we have to play. The first to understand and adopt a heterarchical order model were transnational terrorism and organized crime groups. From there, precisely, it has derived its power to adapt to the complexity of these times and not only survive but grow more robust. But, more recently, heterarchy has reached new frontiers and is now one of the preferred forms of organization of large technology companies, pharmaceutical giants, corporations belonging to the Chinese Communist Party, and even some branches of the North American State. Failing to understand

and incorporate the heterarchy models into organizations could lead to succumbing to liquid risks. In the logic of accelerationism, heterarchies are a natural response to our times. A projection of a few years is enough to convince the most skeptical that Western civilization faces the challenge of survival to liquid risks.

The convergent advance of global criminal regimes and organizations threatens not only the peace of an entire hemisphere but also the founding values of democracy, liberty, and justice akin to the West. On the other hand, heterarchies profoundly alter power relations, which fosters the spiral of risks, adding complexity and uncertainty to the situation. At this point, the first task is to make ourselves aware of what we are facing. In the liquid world, there is no protection due to ignorance; on the contrary, the first victims are usually those who ignore or do not want to see reality.

Where once solid positions were held regarding the value of institutions, the rule of law, or social norms, unexpected or almost unimaginable situations have arisen

13

Liquid elections
or how to hack the system

Elections are the source of legitimacy in democracies and are simultaneously the point in the history of nations from which power emerges. Hence, the interest of liquid organizations aiming to manipulate elections, alter their results, and influence voters's decisions. All over the world, we have heard stories of electoral fraud committed from inside and outside of power. For example, in the 2019 Bolivian elections, the first audits showed the change of the totalization servers at a time when the results were not favorable to Evo Morales, with the purpose of placing him ahead of the other candidates. Recent history has provided evidence of much more sophisticated cases. In Venezuela, the registration of up to four million virtual voters who appear and disappear, according to the conveniences of the National Electoral Council, has been documented. In the 2017 elections for the National Constituent Assembly, *Smartmatic*, a private sector provider of technological support to the electoral body, reported that the totalization included at least one million more votes than those they counted from their platform.

In 2020, when the peak of electoral liquefaction in the United States was reached, there were so many and so complex doubts created around the election that 33% of the voters, according to a survey carried out by five North American universities, had concerns that the result expressed the genuine will of the voters. The United States has as many electoral systems as states in the Union. Based on regional autonomies, each manages its own voting and vote-counting platform. On the other hand, each state has several modalities for early voting, which begins four or five weeks before election day, such as the possibility of voting by mail, which in the midst of the pandemic reached 46% of the total votes cast. However, the most significant concern regarding the electoral results is the threat associated with unofficial online campaigns, many of them promoted not only by countries that are antagonists of the West, such as Russia and China, but also by Western nations interested in promoting disinformation aimed at shaping the voters' electoral decision. The election has become the new battlefield for materializing liquid risks, even more so when power is at stake in the strongest and most influential nation on the planet.

Although how these risks emerge depends on factors that predispose their materialization or are the response to a particular sequence, it is possible to identify some signs linked to them. First, reality is no longer defined by certainties as large gaps of complexity and uncertainty have replaced it. Where there were once solid positions regarding the value of institutions, the rule of law, or social norms, unexpected or almost unimaginable situations have arisen. In an environment of uncertainty, reality is fertile enough to counter-inform, misinform, and falsify the truth, which not only enhances risks but also generates a chaotic environment conducive to making even the impossible begin to look probable. For the process of relativization of the truth, the more interpreters there are, the more signs come between reality and the object, making the ordinary citizen's understanding of the environment more complex, therefore thwarting the possibility of locating oneself in the present and without the ability to predict the immediate future. All this is mixed up with the polarization of the political debate driven by social networks and accelerated by media with extremely high diffusion power.

Uncertainty and chaos exist, not because a *deus ex machina* is pulling the strings or designing and building a reality in one way instead of the other. What lies underneath are organizations that have learned to take advantage of the unpredictability and incomprehension of reality, putting themselves in a position of great strategic advantage over those who perceive the world as a linear succession of causes and effects. Although not all organizations that exploit chaos are criminals, those that do so only for power can be considered as such since they can influence the will of individuals and communities, modifying their perceptions of freedom, democracy, or the vote. They operate like hackers of both societies and how their citizens elect their governments.

The state of democracies is no longer measured based on the strength of their institutions. The multiple opportunities for intervening in electoral processes or the growing social control have become evident worldwide. So much so that each election is not only a business for criminal organizations dedicated to straining the atmosphere of countries at election times. Elections have now become nodal points for the marketing of ideologies through the promotion of non-governmental organizations pervaded by political interests that end up lending themselves to massive social experiments through data manipulation and AI. Something seemingly as simple as the election of candidates through vote counting has become the new and diffuse plane of a war of anonymous and asymmetric threats. They are a complete expression of the liquid risk formation cycle. A risk that can only be mitigated by interrupting its cycle. Hence, social awareness and the leading participation of citizens in electoral processes, even with the State bodies created for this purpose, are essential conditions for elections to be carried out with due guarantees, transparency, fairness, and freedom from threats. If we do not understand the risk of holding elections amid uncertainty, we will lose democracy.

In 1981, Samuel Huntington predicted that the United States would enter a profound moral upheaval beginning in the second decade of the 21st century. This forecast was made based on a study of the sixty-year cycles the United States has supposedly gone through. The last cycle began in 1960. Hence, according to Huntington, 2020 was the year when a new crisis would occur. Many factors suggest that Huntington's prediction was accurate. What is worse is that it is likely that this new crisis may have consequences that we are only beginning to understand. According to Huntington, the American nation is founded on ideals. The problem is that such ideals are unattainable. The distance between what the founders and those in power aimed and what they attained has been a source of social problems. *"In terms of Americans' beliefs, the government is supposed to be egalitarian, participatory, open, noncoercive, and responsive to the demands of individuals and groups. However, no government can be all these things and still be a government."* Although Huntington's thesis is difficult to prove, some political analysts and journalists rely on it to explain the phenomenon of Trump and his rise to power, linking the American moral crisis with the collapse of trust and confidence and a breakdown of the social cohesion of the people that started in 2016.

One of the outcomes of the Democrat's narrative during that campaign was the moral disarming of the people. Citizens were presented with a devastating panorama, arguing that in four years, Trump had weakened the entire country's social fabric, undoing the relationships of trust in the nation. Thus, because of Trump, society has been left in the midst of its deepest orphanhood since the State stopped protecting it. The Democrats' narrative presented a weak and incapable State and a demoralized nation without confidence, for which it was no longer worth fighting because, amid chaos, all individual effort was useless, and what was required then was someone with the ability to sort things out. Citizens were persuaded that society needed a new order directed by the experience of someone with the proper skills. It is obvious that it was an almost utopian hypothesis, given the nature of our globalized, hyperconnected planet imbued with a complexity that prevents restoring any order. The main reason to predict this failure with such assertiveness is that, according to liquid modernity, what prevails is the logic of fluid dynamics, where nothing remains in its place for a long time, and what is new is devalued at such a rate that there is no time left to organize. This is how, over time, demoralization has effectively won battles without fighting them.

David Brooks, a well-known NYT editorialist, published an essay in The Atlantic where he wrote, *"Trump is the final instrument of this [moral] crisis, but the conditions that brought him to power and have made him so dangerous at this moment are decades in the making, and those conditions are not going to disappear, even if he is defeated."* Again, the power of the media was used to demoralize the citizen, diluting his individuality. For these new prophets, what is done no longer matters since the size of the chaos is such that they thought that even if Trump lost the elections, a new model of state would be imposed. The typical American ignores the turn of the democrats towards the empowerment of the Welfare State, which was not presented clearly but was rather sold deceptively, creating the need for it to exist since, in the current reality, *"the cancer of mistrust has spread to all organs"* as Brooks points out. Therefore, it is necessary to recompose society. However, in his conclusions, Brooks is not optimistic about whether a proper solution to the problem of moral upheaval exists on this occasion. Although his pessimism is real, he fails to understand that the moral crisis is not the product of historical cycles typical of North American society. Brooks misses the point that we are in the midst of a planetary process never experienced shaped by non-linear forces. Therefore, it does not adhere to the parameters of a traditional order that can be established from the experience of those who have governed in the past. It is a process that can only be conducted rather than governed. A process that requires a good dose of flexibility and independence without too many cultural ties or feelings of guilt.

Trump obtained a higher vote in 2020 (74.22 million) than the votes he received when he was elected president in 2016 (62.98 million). His offer, *Make America Great Again*, revolved around calling the people to build on the pride of being American and requalify the citizens from the local and not the global. Trump, in his four presidential years, was a wanderer of power. Although he understood the liquid risks he faced and intended to be a dam to contain them, the complex dynamics of anonymous and undetectable threats weighed more than his charisma and political power. His last resort in this battle was never to recognize Biden's victory, to delegitimize him as president. Playing the art of demoralization with the people of the United States, who have grown multiple times over their difficulties and have emerged stronger without losing their freedoms, is not easy to achieve. However, we are in a liquid game, where you neither win nor lose; you are only temporarily ahead or behind.

The study of authoritarian regimes will have to become a topic of global discussion sooner rather than later, not only because of the power they accumulate, the humanitarian crises they cause, and the threats they represent but also because they intentionally generate an imbalance in the world of democracies and an unprecedented challenge to the security of nations, regions, and organizations.

14

Liquid totalitarianism

The Internet, our greatest tool of emancipation, has become the
most dangerous enabler of totalitarianism ever seen.

-Julian Assange

An investigation published by The Economist Intelligence Unit on the state of democracies in 2021 highlighted that 93 of a total of 167 countries included in the research were considered authoritarian or hybrid regimes, while 53 had flawed democracies, some so fragile that *They were not capable of controlling the excesses of their rulers.* The accelerated dynamics of global changes and new information technologies have contributed to satisfying growing social demands but have not been proportionally translated into real changes towards more democratic political systems. To some extent, the trend has been different from what we would have expected. The tools of globalization are being capitalized more skillfully by authoritarian regimes, reinforcing their capabilities not only to maintain power but to vigorously expand it to new territories, both geographical and cultural. The end of the Soviet Union marked the break of a paradigm in dictatorial models. The rise of power, bureaucratization, and iron control over citizens' relationships made the totalitarian states of the past solidify their structures. And this rigidity rendered them unable to compete in a world that was beginning to transform. While Russia in the 1980s was still clinging to the blast furnaces of the Industrial Revolution, the digital revolution of the microchip and reflexive modernity changed the face of the planet. What Fukuyama called *The End of History* was actually a long transition of 30 years in which liberal democracies became sedentary and flabby in the face of the acceleration of reality. The international institutions born from the Second World War are diminished today, incapable of addressing new challenges, and have somewhat become instruments of authoritarian modes. The horrific events of September 2001, to which the United States responded with the War on Terror, was much more than that. It was about the reconfiguration of power in a global expression, no longer obsessed with order but marked by chaos.

Without willing to overstate the regime that President Hugo Chavez built in Venezuela since he was elected president in 1998 (and along with this, the heterogeneous and chaotic set of ideas that supported it, which is known as Chavismo), it could be argued that this ruler transformed Venezuela and, at the same time, devised a program aimed at launching a new model of totalitarianism adapted to the complex and accelerated reality. What had once sunk traditional totalitarianism now, in a kind of jujitsu of history, had returned to dilute and capture the institutions of democracy using, among others, its electoral instruments. This 2.0 version of totalitarianism is no longer rigid but liquid. In it, power is organized in networks, and its unity of purpose focuses on maintaining and expanding it through the means at its disposal. In liquid totalitarianism, there is only one rule and one purpose: Holding power. Therefore, those who share their objectives with those of the totalitarian project will be paid. Understanding how transnational criminal groups, local gangs, and allied governments align under the same principle is not difficult. While it is true that all totalitarianism aims to maintain power, in the liquid version, there are differences.

The most relevant is the organization in heterarchical networks that converge in the unity of purpose. The diversity of organizations and countries that make up a network that converges and, therefore, makes liquid totalitarianism possible have multiple interests. Still, they all contribute in one way or another to sustaining power. Even completely legitimate ones may sometimes align with those heterarchical networks (such would be true for NGOs, unions, and even democratically elected governments).

In these liquid manifestations of totalitarian power, the system assembles and uses other more sophisticated properties to protect and strengthen itself. In the following lines, I examine the most relevant. 1. Early efforts toward breaking the Principle of Alternation in Power, either through referendum or constitutional changes. The government aimed not only to elect the same person to the presidency uninterruptedly but to legalize the perpetuity of the system, maintaining power beyond individual leadership. This happened with Hugo Chávez in Venezuela, who conducted an electoral consultation in 2009 to modify the Constitution and introduce indefinite reelection. A similar process was furthered by Evo Morales in Bolivia. He was willing to be a candidate for a third term, although this option had been denied in a popular referendum, the Supreme Electoral Court, one of the government branches under his control, qualified him as a candidate for the 2019 elections. Although neither Chavez nor Morales are currently presidents of their countries (the former died in 2013), the authoritarian regimes they designed proved successful. 2. Liquid totalitarianism usually simulates that the State encourages the independence of the different branches, as in liberal democracies, so the Legislative, the Judiciary, and the Electoral branches are preserved. However, the Executive has captured all three because it aims to sustain the government in power. 3. Fragmented power is distributed to actors who converge in interests and purposes. Through this distribution, a relationship of a specific actor with the control network is created, and the agreement that underlies this relationship is the actor's tacit agreement that it will be accountable in proportion to the power granted under penalty of repressive actions. Such fragmentation generates internal competition in crime networks, working as a self-regulator of power that could be compared to a criminal system of checks and balances. As long as the network nodes remain in the dynamics of equilibrium and do not conflict with the purposes of totalitarianism, their activities will have a place in the system. And 4. The system's ability to simulate a state of permanent tension between order and chaos conveys the idea that power networks are guarantors of peace. This strategy seeks to discourage any attempt of external intervention on the assumption that if it happens, it will alter a fragile balance, triggering uncontrolled and unpredictable consequences much worse than maintaining the totalitarian status quo. This is the way liquid totalitarianism becomes resilient to adversity and highly flexible. Therefore, it cannot be broken (liquid does not break), given its extremely high adaptation skill. Hence, these systems are resilient to any attempts to fracture the governing coalition, the military, or the repressive groups. Dislodging liquid regimes from power requires a different strategic approach, the stages of which are detailed below. First, it is essential to understand five basic characteristics:

1. The operation substrate is chaos, the area from which it draws energy. Its power is derived from the speed to adapt to emerging phenomena that arise from the complexity of chaos. Liquid totalitarianism is always alert to adjust and take advantage of reality, even in adverse conditions. The pandemic represents a good example. Compared to liberal democracies, authoritarian regimes were more extreme at achieving social control, so it is not a surprise they used the pandemic as a weapon and an argument. Due to their

intimate relationship with chaos, liquid totalitarian systems are not governed by efficiency, hierarchy, or meritocratic principles but by loyalty to the purpose of power.

2. Power in liquid totalitarianism is not static but dynamic; it flows between the multiple actors (nodes) that make up the network. Structures adapt around a gravity center from where decisions are made. The networks have multiple redundant nodes, so if one fails, another takes its position without further disrupting the system

3. Multiple interactions, also known as transfer relationships, occur between network nodes. Hence, learning how these relationships arise is critical to decoding the liquid framework. In this sense, for liquid totalitarianism, the control and manipulation of information are essential components of the system. Transfer relationships cannot be completely public because if they are exposed, the network becomes vulnerable.

4. Liquid totalitarianism, based on adaptive networks, learns through trial and error. Errors or failures usually do not generate major consequences because none of the nodes is critical. This is how their gravity centers can heal themselves and correct deviations that could place the system at risk.

5. One of the favorite tools of liquid power is the construction of narratives to relativize the truth, redirect public opinion, or build enemies. These are well-studied methods in which reality is dismantled and rearranged in favor of the interests of totalitarianism. It is perhaps one of the characteristics inherited from the traditional totalitarian model. Thus, in George Orwell's novel 1984, the Party manipulates language to maintain control over the population. The Party also controls the creation of books, only allowing books that fit the

government's ideology. Orwell was also aware of the ability of the totalitarian State to alter language, stripping words from their original meaning and conferring them a sense that was usually the opposite. So, Orwell coined the term newspeak to designate this language that could diminish the span of thoughts, which would, in turn, shorten their memory. Besides being focused on language, Liquid totalitarianism is re-empowered through information technologies and social networks.

Thus, due to their outstanding adaptation abilities, liquid totalitarianism does not collapse with specific or single actions, even if these are forceful. Therefore, predicting the fall of totalitarianism according to the outcomes of an election, a package of sanctions, the uprising of a few isolated barracks, or a popular insurrection will be a failure mainly because the system can absorb turbulence and recalibrate its gravity center so as not to dismantle it. These complex adaptive systems will only collapse when: 1. A combination of events takes place that, in a mixture of simultaneity and sequence, gives rise to such a failure that it cannot be processed through the power nodes, producing catastrophic and irreversible damage, and 2. The system loses its stressors and relaxes to such a point that its ability to adapt agilely to emerging phenomena is reduced to a critical level, becoming sedentary and slow.

Catastrophic failures are difficult to trigger but not impossible. They are usually a combination of emergent phenomena exploited by system counterforces. To induce a catastrophic failure, the counterforces must analyze in detail the architecture of the network within which the liquid totalitarian system is built and, from there, design a dynamic model of failures that combines nodes, centers of gravity, and transfer relationships. The study of authoritarian regimes will have to become, sooner rather than later, a topic of global discussion, not only because of the power they accumulate, the humanitarian crises they cause, and the threats they represent but because they are intentionally generating an imbalance in the world of democracies and an unprecedented challenge to the security of nations, regions, and organizations. They are models that are not contained in their geographical borders since they need to prey on their environments to ensure the purpose of power.

The case of Syria

After the death of Hafez Al Assad in 2000, with one month remaining before being re-elected, and after 29 years in power, he was succeeded by his son Bashar Al Assad, a doctor specializing in ophthalmology at the Western Eye Hospital in London, because of the death of his older brother Bassel in a traffic accident. In 2011, following the events of the Arab Spring, Bashar led Syria into a civil war, which has not yet ended. Through the liquid models of totalitarianism, he has continued to govern his country, which has become an immense and chaotic gray zone. In the revealing book about the Syrian civil war, *Assad or We Burn the Country: How One Family's Lust for Power Destroyed Syria*, written by the American-Lebanese journalist Sam Dagher, the political-criminal nature of Bashar Al Assad is described in detail, as well as the adaptive capacities of his networks that have allowed him not only to stay in power but to consolidate his ruling and continue to be re-elected as president of Syria. Dagher masterfully synthesizes in three aspects the advice that Assad's closest mentors provided him in relation to how to remain in power during times of crisis. Those pieces of advice convey a clear idea of the adaptability of the new totalitarianism: 1. *Time is on your side, so wait and let it act.* Unlike France or the United States, Syria has no real elections, parliament, or public opinion to deal with. Their leaders come and go, rise and fall, while you remain. 2. *Maneuver, block, confuse, and lie, and always use force, extreme force, when you deem necessary. Ultimately, the West will admire your toughness and perseverance; they love strong men and winners. 3. Always make sure you have elements to leverage yourself and the right cards that allow you to play and hit where it hurts. Eventually, your enemies will come on their knees to negotiate with you.* In May 2021, Bashar was voted for a third time for a new seven-year term in an election disputed by Western nations. Meanwhile, Europe and the United States remain in the dilemma of negotiating to alleviate the humanitarian crisis and destruction that devastates the Syrians. According to the above-quoted report prepared by The Economist Intelligence Unit, the democracy index worldwide decreased by 3.29% between 2010 and 2021, and the trend is downward. It is time to ask ourselves why the world's governments are becoming progressively more authoritarian despite all the promises of freedom accompanying globalization.

In postmodern society, physical force has been replaced by perception, simulation, and influence as the primary means of wielding power.

15

From *The Matrix* to liquid wars

*Did you know that the first Matrix was designed to be a perfect human
world where none suffered, and everyone would be happy?
It was a disaster.*

-Agent Smith – The Matrix

Many of my contemporary movie buff friends were marked by
The Matrix, the trilogy of films directed by the Wachowski
brothers (today sisters, Lily and Julie). The first installment of this
series, released in 1999, narrates the awakening of Neo, the leading
character (Keanu Reeves), to the idea that the world is a simulation
created by a super AI that has managed to dominate humanity.
This film shows how humans are trapped within an imaginary
reality created by these machines. This is an illusory reality that
human beings who live within it do not realize that it is not real.
The Matrix can be conceived of as a free version of the thesis of
French philosopher, intellectual, and theorist of postmodernism
Jean Baudrillard (1929 -2007), whose ideas are summarized in the
opening quote from his book *Simulacra and Simulation* (1981): *The
simulacrum is never what hides the truth, it is the truth that hides the
fact that it does not exist.* The simulacrum is the truth. This quote
from Baudrillard suggests that the reality we perceive may be a
simulacrum and that what we consider to be the truth may actually
be an illusion that hides a more profound, unknown, or even non-

existent reality. This notion aligns with the central theme of *The Matrix*, where it is suggested that the truth must be discovered and challenged to understand reality thoroughly. So, although the phrase itself does not come directly from the referred film, it captures the essence of the philosophy that underlies the series, which explores the idea of simulation, the perception of reality, and the search for a true understanding of reality.

For Baudrillard, reality goes even beyond movies since humanity has discarded the concept of reality and made the simulacrum its truth. Thus, truth becomes subjective since it is constructed from what is simulated, and as with any simulation, it can be shaped, reshaped, altered, or arbitrarily interpreted by anyone. We end up believing that reality is a version narrated from the interests of third parties. The complex and disturbing thing about the simulation is that it expresses the domination exercised by those who can impose their own stories. This vision of power is not new; a century ago, Antonio Gramsci argued that every power structure created its own superstructure based on ideology. This was transmitted and perpetuated through institutions, culture, art, family, and laws, among other soft elements of society. Today, ideology has mutated into more liquid forms, becoming narratives of power that no longer require as much structure since social networks and web media are enough to make them sustainable, or in the words of Jason P. Lowery in his book *Softwar*, they constitute abstract power, as opposed to physical power.

In postmodern society, the physical force has been replaced by perception, simulation, and influence as the primary means of wielding power. In some ways, those who can tell a compelling story and gain willing followers can be as influential and deterrent as brute force. In the evolution of civilization, a fundamental change has occurred in how power is wielded. In the past, physical force was the primary tool to persuade someone to believe or do anything.

However, the current break is based on a deconstruction of reality that, by replacing it with its simulation, modifies the perception of power, which can also be simulated. If there are adequate means to spread out the simulation, power is simultaneously built. This perception, which we can call abstract power, is manifested through the narrative capacity of those who wield power. Its application has gained ground as a subtle but highly effective strategy to build and strengthen leadership and sustain increasingly less democratic governments at the head of the States.

We cannot deny that abstract power exists. However, this is a very different power from physical power. Being abstract, power becomes liquid and intangible but with authentic effects. In fact, abstract power can generate dysfunctions that can lead to war. According to Lowery, abstract power has the following main characteristics: i) It is not self-evident or self-legitimizing, meaning it cannot be recognized using intuition alone. ii) It is not independently verifiable; iii) It is systematically endogenous to the belief system of a population; in fact, it needs the sympathy of its population; iv) It cannot be excessively restricted since it depends on the collective imagination; v) It can be modified or undone, since being part of a simulation it has no consequences in the physical world; vi) Imposes limits on the amount of power you can exercise with it; vii) In essence, it is not attributable to anyone, because, first of all, it is made of ideas, which makes it very difficult to assess it as a threat, much less organize against it; viii) It does not use physical energy.

Physical power can, in turn, be used to legitimize or delegitimize abstract power. In the case of legitimization, it acts as a reinforcement to blur the border between the imaginary and the real. This power disruption occurs, for example, with selective repression in autocratic governments. By spreading the narrative of torture, the population is dissuaded from rebelling against the system. The most sophisticated expression of abstract power in these regimes is self-censorship. Some citizens go to the extreme of constraining themselves in the expression of their words (and even their thoughts) in exchange for not being considered an enemy and thus becoming victims of persecution.

Abstract power exercised through the narratives of autocracies also has an old counterbalance. It is about the historic confrontation of good against evil and, in its most human and updated version, in the fight for freedom. This is how heroes and their epics are born to liberate people. The archetypal stories of the hero in training tell of the multiple battles in which he overcomes obstacles. At the same time, these obstacles are transformed into small victories and great learnings; they also become their own experience of inner growth until reaching the final fight in which the oppressor is defeated, thus defeating evil and achieving freedom. The hero's story adapted to the leader and converted into a narrative of victory is the most convincing expression of the process of building abstract power.

Abstract power today has many other manifestations besides politics. It is used in the marketing world, where companies compete not only based on the quality of their products but also on their ability to influence consumer perception. Advertising strategies are based on creating a brand image and generating trust in consumers, which in turn drives sales. For example, brands like Apple have used the perception of innovation and elegant design to exert a powerful appeal to consumers. The function of marketing is to attribute power to the brand, creating a unique and indispensable narrative since it would be impossible to enter a new dimension of reality without it. For its part, the digital age and social networks have become amplifiers of abstract power and its enveloping influence. Today, platforms like "X" (formerly known as Twitter), Facebook, TikTok, or Instagram allow users to communicate directly with large audiences and shape public opinion. Online influencers and opinion leaders significantly impact topics ranging from politics to pop culture. Networks have become an additional terrain for the propagation of narratives and the power struggle. It is no coincidence that Elon Musk has invested a significant part of his fortune in acquiring Twitter when this platform did not represent a profitable business in economic terms. Still, it did in the abstract plane of power.

Returning to Lowery's thesis in *Softwar*, which is actually about the security advantages of Bitcoin and its unique power in the cyber world, he argues that we are entering a stage in which all power will end up being abstract, so wars will no longer be fought on the kinetic plane. Still, everything will occur in the cyber domain. In such a dematerialized territory, the blockchain is an equalizing power representing the maximum level of security a system can have. Hence, it will become a kind of real-world atomic bomb, which is used, first of all, to deter others from attacking you since it would represent mutual annihilation.

In one of the most memorable scenes of *The Matrix*, Neo, the leading character, is confronted by Morpheus, a rebel in the simulated world, who presents him with a dilemma. Morpheus asks Neo to choose one of two pills he holds in his hand, one blue and one red. The red pill represents an uncertain future: it would liberate him from the enslaving control of the dream world generated by AI and allow him to escape to the real world. But living the truth of reality is a more complex and difficult task. The blue pill represents a beautiful prison: it would take you back to ignorance, living in confined comfort, without need or fear, within the simulated reality of the Matrix. As Morpheus describes it: *You take the blue pill... the story ends, wake up in bed, and believe whatever you want. You take the red pill... you stay in Wonderland, and I show you how deep the rabbit hole is.* Neo chooses the red pill and joins the rebellion. In this postmodern society, almost no one dares to take the red

141

pill and accept reality. Abstract power, through its seductive and addictive simulation, has become the fundamental instrument for those seeking domination. The ability to tell a compelling story and gain followers can be as influential as brute force. Ultimately, we must be aware of how abstract power is used and how narratives have become a tool to shape our perception of the world. Only through a higher level of consciousness can we live and, I would say, endure reality. Otherwise, we will end up becoming domesticated sheep living in the Matrix. But changing the world in its physical dimension requires, at some point, an additional effort. Although the simulation is a high-powered tool for creating the environment, the real impact on lives and power relationships emerges from larger-scale conflicts, although no longer necessarily or exclusively conventional in nature. It is here that a type of liquid war advances on the planet.

In May 2023, Pope Francis warned of the risk of humanity's "self-destruction" due to what he called the "Third World War in pieces." It was not the first time the Pope had referenced the Third World War; I had heard it several times. What caught my attention was the expression in pieces, which I will use as a starting point to develop some ideas about the nature of the new conflicts, known as hybrids, which are part of my vision of liquid risks.

The notion of war in pieces is itself challenging. This is not a conventional conflict fought on a defined terrain and with a specific objective. Instead, it is a fragmented, discontinuous confrontation that occurs on multiple levels and is of such complexity that it is not understandable without a deep analysis. War in pieces could resemble hybrid conflicts that are usually asymmetric and characterized by the mixture of traditional elements of war with non-military and subversive methods; however, this goes further. Assuming my bias, I would dare to define it as a *liquid war*. The definition of liquid wars is not as widely known as other concepts related to war conflicts and does not have an established agreement in the academic or military field. Some authors have used the term to describe a type of confrontation in networks characterized by its fluidity, adaptability, and lack of traditional structure. This concept is often associated with modern wars being less predictable and more changeable than conventional ones. Liquid wars involve various elements such as uncertainty, complexity, power asymmetry, and the heterarchical order of the conflicting parties, in which actors can rapidly shift tactics and strategies to adapt to quickly changing circumstances. These conflicts are difficult to foresee and manage due to their elusive nature. They are often fought on multiple fronts, which can include the physical battlefield, cyberspace, culture, psyche, and, of course, information manipulation.

Due to the fluid and changing nature of liquid conflicts, it is tough to assess their impacts; however, they are forceful and have devastating effects in reality. A prominent example of war in pieces, which can be understood as liquid, is mass migration as an instrument of destabilization of countries. Today, it is present throughout the entire planet. It confronts civilians, compromises institutions, generates extreme polarization, implies the diversion of resources, and puts the sovereignty of nations at risk, in addition to being a human drama with profound consequences.

Information can also be used as a weapon to fight liquid wars. It can be aimed at changing the beliefs and attitudes of the population progressively. Constant and subtle exposure to messages and narratives designed to influence how reality is perceived means that people may adopt perspectives they did not have before or that their beliefs may get radicalized. For example, the UK Counter Terrorism Internet Referral Unit declared that there had been *an unprecedented 12-fold increase in hateful social media content*. I have also referred to the wars of demoralization as a subcategory in the cultural war, and that goes directly to disarming the individual from within, to paralyze him and thus steal his own energies to defend himself from attacks.

There has been some agreement among certain analysts that the first transition war between the hybrid and the liquid modes was the one declared against terrorism by George W. Bush after the fateful attacks of September 11, 2001. It was a conflict against an invisible, ubiquitous, and fractalized enemy. A war that developed under the cover of misinformation that took advantage of the nascent digital revolution. It was a war that dissolved 20 years later, in 2021, when the North American troops left Afghanistan, leaving behind a region as chaotic or more chaotic than when they arrived.

Liquid wars are fought on a vast spectrum, from the borders of nations to the psyche of individuals. There is no longer any space for peace or truce in these new conflicts. Therefore, our conscience is the last barrier to protect us against these new threats. In this sense, cognitive security, in the context of this war, can be defined as the field for preserving peace, freedom, democracy, and social cohesion. This is an unprecedented challenge, so creating and deploying a comprehensive strategy that educates, promotes critical thinking, uses protective technologies, establishes policies, and promotes a culture of responsibility is necessary. Only through a holistic and collaborative approach can we successfully face the challenge of simultaneously protecting individuals' minds, physical borders, and wills in a society that, not because it has more information, becomes less vulnerable.

The domain of cognitive security is the development of practical methodologies for defense against social engineering threats (developed by the enemy), which aim to manipulate and cause harm to people and organizations. There is, however, another domain of cognitive security. It refers to the means of prevention, protection, and planning against the processes of transforming information as a weapon to distort perceptions about specific topics that have become the object of disinformation and propaganda. At this level, cognitive security becomes the closest layer of protection for the individual, and strengthening cognitive security is the aim of a liquid risk management system whose efforts are the identification and dismantling of intangible threats created to manipulate information from the level of the psyche, leaving us without the ability to reason. A liquid risk management system needs to defend the individual from disinformation campaigns.

The purpose of information used as a weapon is to change the beliefs and attitudes of the population gradually and, from there, promote behaviors that favor the interests of the designer or intellectual author of the attack. In the past, cognitive security was seen as a science fiction topic since there were many doubts about the capabilities of information systems to manipulate people so profoundly. Still, with the tremendous advances in AI and machine learning today, powerful simulations and deep fake tools can convince even the most skeptical.

The leap of cognitive security from the field of computing to the real world of the citizen is becoming one of the most critical challenges in social risk management. In this sense, events such as elections, vaccination campaigns, or the approval of laws are now new layers of an information war translated into extreme polarization and the struggle to win in any way the mind and will of the individuals. The challenge is to make cognitive security an applicable field, with practices that range from the individual to organizations and society. For this, it is essential, first of all, that governments become aware of the nature of these risks so they can turn to design innovative institutions and cultures to contain and mitigate such risks. Once again, we have arrived at a new expression of the Risk Society, in which we have created significant threats to our survival, and we have not yet developed the means even to realize their power. This is where cognitive security has a place, and I am convinced it will be a concept that will increasingly be present in discussions about protecting ourselves from liquid risks.

...it is not the security of the static and predictable that will make organizations highly reliable; it is precisely the awareness of complexity that will give particular shape to the leadership, structure, culture, and strategy to operate successfully against liquid risks

16

Catastrophism: the vector of intimidation

For since by man came death, by man came also
the resurrection of the dead

-Paul - Corinthians 15:21

The Judeo-Christian tradition is pervaded with catastrophic and apocalyptic ideas. This attitude could be attributed to our early exposure to the Book of Revelation (Apokalipsis), the last book of the New Testament, that left an imprint that, one day, a catastrophic event will wipe out the world and all the living beings on Earth, including man. A new flood, the horrific explosion of a supervolcano, a horrendous quake, or an unimaginable series of natural disasters will arrive as universal punishment for our species' repeated wrongdoings, interpreted as sacrilegious sins or acts of disobedience to God. The Western culture has inherited the concept of damnation. Irremediable times will arrive, and our fears of a gloomy end of the world will materialize.

Thousands of years later, fear makes us all vulnerable to storytellers who enjoy instilling it in their readers. We fall for apocalyptic narratives (and their metaphors), a term I choose to designate any natural or human-made catastrophes, including anything from the most extreme natural events to the most likely human-made threat and everything in between. Although we can be lured by stories whose plots are catastrophes, we fear that the apocalyptic narratives might become reality someday. Some people have realized that awakening, fostering, and shaping these fears may model our thoughts and decisions, similar to exercising a *supernatural* power. The common sense question would be: Do apocalyptic risks really threaten our times? Or, has instead the narrative used catastrophism as an instrument to trigger and spur our fears, transforming them into liquid risks?

Although risks are intrinsic to the complexity we are immersed in, liquid risks do not determine the inevitable materialization of a catastrophic reality. All risk belongs to the territory of the probable. There is always the possibility that they will materialize and generate unwanted impacts or that this possibility never happens. Hence, risk per se is not an a *priori* condemnation that leads us to live in a world drowned in the unpredictability of times. The probability for risks to materialize is primarily determined by the quality of the threat and the power of liquid organizations to exploit the vulnerabilities of potential victims. In the case of emerging risks, many of the liquid risks are added to the addictive power that such threats constitute, and that can be used to allure those with low levels of awareness.

Let us consider global warming. Sure, it is a man-made disaster grounded on scientific evidence. Over the last five decades, the story alleges that humans are living an accelerated process of destroying the planet's natural resources. Although we have already caused irreversible damage, if we do not do something soon, if the trend is not timely and adequately reversed, humanity will not be saved. It is a lose-lose dilemma because, for the group of green devotees, any action has the risk of being perceived as being less than what is needed to save ourselves. And if humanity decides to inaction, humans shall be blamed as criminal predators of the Earth's renewable natural resources. Perhaps half a century is a short time to validate this hypothesis of environmental catastrophe, but what is certain is that the apocalypse has not arrived yet and that the same technology that scares us could, in most unexpected ways, eventually provide us with a solution to more efficiently deal with the problem.

Catastrophism can be used as a vector of intimidation in society. It seeks to paralyze (not mobilize) people through fear and delegate decision-making on global issues. It is not about denying the facts that reveal climate change; the risk arises when the use of certain types of energy, the industrial use of some materials, or the exploitation of the land for agricultural activities are manipulated through political agendas by imposing visions—environmentalists above the needs or opportunities of society. Like most of the risks of the liquid world, catastrophism contains its own paradox: If we are condemned to live on a damaged planet, what is the point of working to reduce greenhouse gas emissions? Of the first five risks with the highest probabilities and impacts published by the World Economic Forum in its *2022 Global Risks Report*, four correspond to the environmental category, and only the pandemic risk appears in the social category. Other risks, such as involuntary migrations or social conflict and civil wars, appear much lower in order, to mention two that have been present in recent years and have significantly affected millions of people and nations of various continents. If we cannot do much to stop threats, we can work on the vulnerability side, starting with raising awareness of the risks. To do this, it is helpful to take Robert S. Kaplan and Anette Mikes' classification of risks in *Framework for Managing Risks* and deconstruct the sense of inevitability contained in the catastrophic narrative:

- **Preventable Risks:** These are the internal risks of an organization. They are controllable and can be mitigated, eliminated, or avoided. These risks include illegal, unethical, inappropriate, or incorrect actions. The best way to manage these risks is through active prevention. That is, monitoring and guiding people and their decisions toward desired norms.

- **External Risks:** arise from events outside the organization and beyond its control. Sources of these risks include natural disasters, political changes, or large macroeconomic swings. These types of risks require a different approach. Since they are not preventable, the focus must be on identifying them and planning to reduce the severity of their impacts.

- **Strategy Risks:** These are the risks an organization is willing to accept to obtain the maximum benefit as it pursues its objectives. A bank takes the risk of lending money to its customers because, if it does it right, it can maximize its profits. A strategy that expects high returns involves proportionate risks. Therefore, managing strategy risks requires a system designed to minimize the chances that specific risks will materialize. The idea is not to prevent organizations from taking risks through these systems; quite the opposite, it is about providing them with a safety net so they can take risks more confidently.

According to the author's risk categorization, there is a human dimension to the environmental risk of climate change that would be preventable (for instance, the deforestation of the Amazon forest and the destruction of its ecosystem). Something similar happened during the 45 years of the Cold War and the risk of using atomic weapons of mass destruction. Being a preventable risk, both the United States and the USSR used it in their power agendas to convince the world that nuclear destruction would be a matter over which there was no control once the first rocket with a nuclear warhead was launched, making it inevitable. From there, risk was used as a vector of intimidation (and terror) to strategically capitalize on the political and military polarization of the planet. It is worth noting that, in general, the enhancing component of catastrophism that cannot be ignored is the incorporation of liquid narratives. In the world of infinite possibilities, infinite versions of the same ultra-risk can be narrated by segmenting audiences and using a wide-spectrum strategy, from the most direct ones operating on irrational fear to other very sophisticated ones aimed at more skeptical audiences. Although catastrophism has historically been used as a strategy to manipulate the masses, this is in itself a form of liquid risk linked to the means used to make it seem inevitable.

In the liquid world, the debates have globalized and accelerated at the same pace as the risks, and the result has not been consensus but rather polarization. In the polarized political arena, positions become trenches, and those who engage in the debates throw their arguments as darts, each standing on their own narrative platform. This is where catastrophic visions seem to aim, shaking the fibers of fear. It does not appear that this dynamic of accelerated complexity will change shortly since we are only now entering. Nor is it likely that the strategy of catastrophism will stop being used as a vector of intimidation in the narratives of power because it has demonstrated its efficiency in polarizing scenarios. Here, the questions are: Who are those intimidated, and who are those who use the strategy of catastrophism? Are the people intimidated by those in power? In some cases, the answer is affirmative. But, other times, it may well be that catastrophism has arisen spontaneously, time and again, in history. The reason would be that humans have a propensity to pessimism that leads some people to amplify even inconceivable extremes of the threats they face or perceive. One of these extreme scenarios is the apocalypse of the catastrophist. At this point, the unavoidable question seems to be: What other options remain besides raising awareness about catastrophic visions of risks? Perhaps the answer lies in the same paradox of liquid risks. In the world of infinite possibilities, we have run out of answers to mitigate them, or should we rethink the way we have been viewing the world and its realities and thus develop a new set of solutions?

17

Living with an artificial alien

Software is eating the world, but AI is going to eat software.

-Jensen Huang – Nvidia CEO

In preceding chapters, we have argued that, in current times, everything around us is undergoing an accelerated change that leaves obsolete references from the past. Recent Artificial Intelligence (AI) developments are not immune to this change. On the contrary, AI is becoming one of the most important backbones of our transition to a new form of future. The developments I am referring to have been defined as generative artificial intelligence. This term includes algorithms capable of creating new content in text, images, videos, audio, and code. The sheer potential of generative AI to understand the instructions (prompts) that humans give it in natural language has left users in awe. Programs like Chat GPT or Gemini (from Google), based on Large Language Models (LLMs), must be previously trained with vast information. Although LLMs understand natural language, they also have the ability to learn and understand the grammar of molecules, programming codes, the images produced by an MRI device, and endless categories of information. This novel aspect of AI has made it so powerful and attractive to the markets. For example, in January 2023, just over a month after being launched by Open AI, the Chat GPT chatbot reached a user base of 100 million.

What is surprising is that uncertainty does not decrease despite the vast amount of information we have access to. In some way, this postmodernity enhanced by AI is a higher stage on which liquid risks are formed and developed, generated by feedback processes between uncertainty and complexity, which are difficult to identify and even more challenging to mitigate. Our era has tried to manage these risks through tools such as data science and analytics. Some even believe that AI constitutes the most powerful solution to mitigate the dangers of the liquid world. However, we have created a reality of intrinsic risks that cannot be resolved by knowing more. In this sense, AI has become one of the holy grails of risks considered falsely epistemological. The amazing data processing and storage capabilities, increasingly cheaper and more accessible, have transformed algorithms into a kind of formula for the alchemy of digital civilization, which undoubtedly grants extraordinary power to those who know and operate these technologies. But there is no formula to break the paradox of uncertainty versus access to information. This paradox underscores the complexity of managing risks in the AI era, returning us to the intuition that uncertainty is intrinsic to the system and, therefore, impossible to resolve, which can be considered analogous (at the macro level) to the Uncertainty Principle that the physicist Werner Heisenberg proposed in 1927 (for the subatomic level), referring to the fact that it is not possible to determine with precision and simultaneity the position and momentum of a particle.

Residual liquid risk

In the case of liquid risks, an uncertainty principle could be defined, making it impossible for this risk to be completely mitigated. This reinforces the intuition that the risks generated from the complex, accelerated, and individualized world of postmodernity carry a condition that limits their mitigation. This non-mitigable margin would be the one on which we must raise awareness and modify behaviors since we tend to believe that these risks do not exist and that, therefore, the reality enhanced by AI will be harmless. I take the ideas from Mustafa Suleyman, a British researcher and founder of DeepMind, a company dedicated to the development of artificial intelligence, and the former CEO of Inflection AI. Suleyman argues in his book *The Coming Wave* that we are facing a new technological revolution of global reach that will profoundly change everyone's lives. The effect of that change can be luminous and a blessing to humanity or terribly dark and destructive. The possibility of taking one course or another will depend mainly on whether leaders in all areas of our societies have the capacity (and the will) to contain these new and powerful forces. The risks derived from this transformation of humanity are entirely liquid. In fact, the combination of power, complexity, and expansion of AI under the control of malicious actors, individual or collective, associated or not with authoritarian or totalitarian States, has the potential to generate a wide range of liquid risks (see Table 1). Although we can assume that we can moderate these risks to make them tolerable, we must consider that they are installed in the very fabric of modern societies. Only the decision to become fully aware and determined to leadership will lead us to a future with more security and certainty. Indeed, if we consider it thoroughly, AI has all the characteristics of a liquid risk. It arises as a product of a complex world that we do not understand, it generates uncertainty about its expansive power, and although it can answer many questions, it does not necessarily clear up our doubts about the future; on the contrary, it makes it unpredictable; and although AI can be conceived as a technological risk, it has an impact on multiple areas.

AI as a liquid risk

One of the biggest fears generated by AI is that the time will come - which for futurist Ray Kurzweil is almost a fact - when it will surpass human capacity in terms of general intelligence. Kurzweil defined that moment, which we may not be entirely able to anticipate, as the technological singularity. At this point, a super-intelligent AI could make decisions that are harmful to humans, either by accident or by intention. Some experts argue that an advanced AI could develop a *consciousness* of its own and that it would be difficult or impossible to control or stop once it reaches this level. The singularity could be a first level of alert for that limit. But it isn't easy to recognize when technological development will get there if it has not already reached that point, and humans do not know because the AI is concealing it. However, we do not need to reach the singularity for AI to reach a level where it will surpass the capability of any human. The experts in the field have defined this level as Artificial General Intelligence (AGI). Sam Altman, CEO of Open AI, has said that he believes that AGI will possibly be built in the *"reasonably close-ish future."* However, he also felt that AGI's impact on the world and jobs would be considerably smaller than we are imagining right now. Regarding the risks derived from AI, Altman, Suleyman, and many others in the field believe these are complex and difficult to contain. Suppose AI develops self-awareness, which, according to Suleyman, is likely to occur relatively quickly. In that case, we will be talking about an intelligent entity different (and superior) to the human being, with the ability to perceive itself as an independent being. If we ever reach such a situation, we would face a very liquid risk constructed entirely by humans, just like the nuclear bomb, but on this occasion, with very low possibilities of containment since the AI would have its own "free will" to protect itself from any human attempt to constrain it or harm it. We would then be at the mercy of

158

the self-coded algorithms since the AI might conclude that humans represent a threat to their own existence. However, existential risks like those described are neither the most likely nor the most dangerous at present.

Post-truth, misinformation, and the techno-panopticon

One of the most important liquid risks indicated in the table below is related to the ability of AI to manipulate information, creating what has been defined as *post-truth*. In times of AI, what is stated in a text may no longer be false. Still images, audio or video recordings, processed with algorithms capable of *deep fake*, can emulate the voices, sounds, and pictures of places and people with such fidelity that they become indistinguishable from the real thing. AI, reinforced by sophisticated facial recognition algorithms and other biometric data, integrated into social networks and in devices that have become part of our lives, such as smartphones or word processors, increases the risk (already referred to in this book) that the world of the near future will become a ubiquitous *techno-panopticon* with formidable capabilities for surveillance and control of the public and private lives of individuals. This risk will be more significant in authoritarian States, which can implement models of social control or surveillance and limit individual freedoms that will be even more sophisticated and effective than those they had recently implemented. In addition to increasing the power asymmetry gap, all of this could add superhuman traits to totalitarian leadership. Under these perspectives, it does not seem like a whim that some experts are asking for a pause on new AI developments, seeking more time to advance and reinforce efforts to align AI with reality and human values. This globality mainly includes humanity, nature, and society. However, it is difficult to do so due to the open, distributed, and collaborative nature that AI has had, mainly due to policies promoted by *OpenAI*. Furthermore, if only the liberal and fully democratic States agree to a moratorium but the outlaw States, or simply the antagonists of the West, do not comply, this could grant a technological advantage to these States, creating a new threat for the West.

It is essential to understand that AI has the potential to contribute in a formidable way to the generation of large amounts of knowledge and thus help us solve complex problems. However, we cannot ignore the fact that there is a risk that the gap between what we know and what we do not know will widen. As we increasingly rely on AI to process and analyze large amounts of data, we may lose the ability to understand and contextualize information. Instead of developing our own capacity for reasoning and critical analysis, we would depend too much on the solutions that AI offers us, solutions whose profound or ultimate reasons we may ignore. In the short term, we may find that our ability to understand the world around us has been undermined, and this would place us in a lower band of expertise that would make us vulnerable to new kinds of risks. Despite doubts about the risks linked to AI, I do not intend to construct a catastrophic forecast for this category of threats. Not only because we are still early in the technological development curve, which leads us to overestimate the dimensions of the risk, but also because, in the past, we have experienced situations that put us at an existential crossroads, and we learned to moderate them or live with them. We have to trust our human nature. We must, therefore, resist our propensity to anticipate highly disruptive scenarios that, at the same time, lead us to imagine dystopian worlds a la *Terminator* instead of other more hopeful, kinder, and less artificial scenarios.

Works like Suleyman's book leave the reader with a feeling of optimism because although our ability to stop (or postpone) the development of AI and related technologies is a formidable task, there is the possibility of containing and leading the expansion in the right direction. An example of this is nuclear energy. Since 1945, the development of nuclear and thermonuclear weapons has evolved significantly, and strategies such as deterrence, based on the principle of mutually assured destruction or MAD, have allowed us to contain the risks of nuclear conflagration. However, in parallel, we have been able to direct nuclear technology towards peaceful purposes such as, for example, the development of nuclear reactors that have been key to supplying electricity to large urban centers. The wise management of this technology has helped us avoid its worst consequences, one of which is self-destruction. It is worth highlighting here that AI is increasingly accessible to people, and the probability of its spread for unethical purposes is more significant than in the case of atomic weapons, which means that these risks can spread quickly, and the task of containment will require a responsible approach and multinational AI regulation and governance strategies. So, a new question arises: How do we guarantee containment capacity? The response has several levels and ranges from the individual's awareness of undetectable threats through modifying certain corporate behaviors linked to risk appetite to designing highly reliable organizations prepared to operate and be successful amid complexity and adversity.

AI and its role in containment

Since I began studying liquid risks arising from AI, I have maintained that the containment of AI risks will be achieved with the help of AI itself. That is, it should be possible to contain risks arising from AI design flaws (such as problems in algorithm code) or malicious use of AI with the help of increasingly AI-powered

161

remediation and robust containment tools. However, this cannot be seen as a simple relationship between machines where there are some tools or algorithms at the service of the well-being of humanity that help man keep AI under his control, and there are other perverse machines that are used for dark and malicious purposes. The realm of AI is extraordinarily heterarchical, and power structures are difficult to identify. Therefore, the human factor will remain essential if we intend to advance any containment strategy. So, it is most likely that humans will develop mixed institutional arrangements involving humans and AI that will play a key role in containing AI. This idea leads me to refer again to the containment (deterrence) model that was implemented during the Cold War when the two antagonistic sides deterred each other through what was known as the threat of mutual destruction or MAD. Given the heterarchical way AI is being deployed, a balance analogous to the one achieved with MAD will not be possible regarding AI. At the time, the nuclear containment strategy had intimidation as its primary objective to avoid mutual destruction, which generated a passive and moderately stable equilibrium that could provide a predictable future. With AI, the game looks very different. In this case, we will try to accelerate development to be at least one step ahead of the threat, or vice versa, the threat ahead of containment. However, the equilibrium in this case will be much more active and unstable, which will not ensure a predictable future. Therefore, the uncertainty gap can remain open indefinitely, making risk always present. An example taken from genetic engineering could reproduce a similar condition, although with different consequences. I am referring to the destructive power that can be achieved by developing new viruses and bacteria of rapid spread and lethality that would be difficult to contain. Beyond considerations about whether COVID-19 was a laboratory creation or emerged spontaneously, the containment tool that was the vaccine took ten months to be available in its final experimental phase. A threat against humanity from AI could never be contained if we first needed to experiment for ten months to find a solution.

AI and the risk of extinction

In his book *Superintelligence*, Nick Bostrom poses the crucial question regarding AI: *If future superhuman artificial intelligence becomes the biggest event in human history, how can we ensure that it is not the last?* The question implies that AI is a double-edged sword in which the risk of extinction of *Homo Sapiens* is inherent. On the one hand, it can solve humanity's problems; on the other, it can become the instrument that will obliterate our species. However, and despite Bostrom's complex analysis, his proposal is reduced to two relatively simple aspects: i) To strategically analyze the problems we need to solve concerning risk, and ii) To group those individuals who have demonstrated a true philanthropic and morally acceptable interest in leading and containing the forces of this superintelligence.

AI is no longer a matter of technology. There is a consensus around the future availability of superintelligence. The Internet is the substrate on which this capacity is developed, as it is an infinite source of information. Likewise, data processing speeds are not a problem, even more so when quantum computing is a reality. However, some limitations persist in programming languages for the creation of superintelligent algorithms with the possibility of self-coding according to the problem they must solve, but this does not seem like a real limitation if we consider what exists today; the results are astonishing, and computer scientists have shown their perplexity on more than one occasion in the face of "unexpected" responses from AI systems:

Risks	Description	Potential impacts
Superintelligence and Self-Aware AI	While still theoretical, AI systems becoming self-aware and surpassing human intelligence is a topic of debate and is considered the highest risk if uncontrolled.	Extinction of the human race. Self-built AI protection to avoid constraints from human programming. AI decisions may not align with human ethics.
Critical infrastructure failure	Hackers can attack critical infrastructure using sophisticated AI-empowered tools. However, AI can enhance resilience by rapidly identifying threats and responding intelligently.	Electric power, water, telecom, airports, and supply chain interruptions. Public services collapse. Unpredictable disruptions of critical services due to AI assumptions with no human intervention.
Weapons Automatization	The development of autonomous weapons powered by AI raises ethical and safety concerns. These weapons could operate without human oversight, leading to unintended consequences.	Uncontrolled human casualties originated from non-human conflicts.
Information manipulation	AI-generated deepfakes can convincingly manipulate audio, video, and images, leading to misinformation, identity theft, and privacy violations. These synthetic media can deceive individuals or spread false narratives.	Disinformation, reputational risks, relativization of truth, Infowars. Distortion of reality, information bubbles, knowledge compartment.
Privacy violations	AI systems often process vast amounts of personal data, raising privacy concerns.	Access and exposure of non-public or personal information.
Market volatility	AI-driven trading algorithms can contribute to market instability. Rapid decision-making by AI systems can amplify market fluctuations.	Sudden and unpredictable macroeconomic changes due to the ripple effects of interconnected stock markets.
Accountability and responsibility	AI systems often operate as "black boxes," making it challenging to understand their decision-making process.	Human accountability gets lost or is seriously undermined in systems that depend on AI.

Risks	Description	Potential impacts
Bias and Discrimination	Ensuring fairness and addressing bias is critical to avoid unintended discrimination. Algorithms can introduce bias, creating some types of discrimination.	Biased training data can lead to discriminatory AI outcomes. Lack of transparency leads to uncertainty about how AI reaches its conclusions, making it challenging to explain its decisions.
Job Displacement	As AI technology is adopted across various industries and functions, there is an increasing risk of job displacement.	Loss of human jobs. Displacement of less trained people to lower scales of income. Increased burden on welfare.
Copyright	Creating content based on patterns and relationships in data is increasingly used in creative industries.	Legal implications regarding copyright infringement and ownership of AI-generated works remain unclear.
Cybersecurity	As AI becomes more sophisticated, cyber threats evolve in complexity. Skilled cybercriminals can use AI tools to craft personalized spear-phishing messages.	Traditional security systems may struggle against cyber-attacks, leaving organizations vulnerable

Table 1: Critical Risks Linked to AI   Source: Author's compilation

The strategic approach to the *problem* of AI as an intrinsic risk is summarized in the probability that a superintelligence will emerge with consciousness and will of its own, hyperconnected and capable of making decisions harmful to people. This could happen if an AI that has been given an order that involves a maximization task persists on a logical inference path and furthers it to an extreme in which moral or ethical considerations are relegated to a lower level, and criteria of another order prevail; such as ideological, racial, religious, political or even purely economic (the example of *office clips*).

Another aspect that demands in-depth analysis is the liquid risk that AI confers enormous intelligence advantages to the sectors that own and control it, which would turn them into privileged members of a superior class. In the long run, this could lead to a society compartmentalized according to levels of mastery over AI and related technologies, such as quantum computing or nuclear fusion. Although this threat may have been present in previous technological revolutions, on this occasion and due to accelerated progress, the gradient factor may lose continuity and generate real gaps between different human groups. This idea reminds me of the accelerationists of Zelasny's in *Lord of Light*.

I understand Nick Bostrom when he points to human beings as the center of gravity to de-escalate the risks inherent in AI. In some way, it is my approach to liquid risks. It is us, from our own nature and in full awareness of preservation as a species, who must draw the limits of containment, and to achieve it, we need to organize the best and with the best intentions. On this occasion, like no other in the past, both conditions are essential: *those who are most qualified with the best intentions.*

However, it is worth noting that containment is not equivalent to a ban. Containing is a much more sophisticated task that, in addition to establishing policies to demarcate ground rules, agrees on criteria to move forward and thus channel the energies of creation, which, if not well understood, will quickly overflow any ill-conceived or arbitrary dam that gets in the way. Prohibiting is conventionally the easiest and most expensive measure in risk management. Even more so in the face of uncertain and complex risks. In any case, the priority mission of containment in AI is security.

In summary, the development of AI requires great care. We need to guarantee awareness, transparency, responsibility, and timely activation capabilities for containment to maximize its positive impact. At the same time, we will have to create early warnings to minimize their risks. Continuous research, development with ethical principles, and thoughtful regulation must contribute to building a future in which AI has the good of humanity as its axis.

So far, we cannot underestimate the quality of the advances of AI in medicine, engineering, and science, among other fields that have enhanced their analysis capabilities, which in turn have accelerated the number of discoveries and the quality of decision-making in the face of highly complex realities. Something wonderful and surprising is that AI has elevated creativity in the world of the arts and is increasing the accessibility of information to the ordinary citizen. Today, AI-powered translation services are breaking down language barriers and expanding communication globally.

Just as postmodernism emerged as a critical expression of rationalism and in the search for answers to the classic and solid deterministic world that developed from the precepts of the Enlightenment, it would be not delusional to conceive of that the current explosion of AI, coming at us like a wave (as Suleyman argues), we may be underestimating the strength of the AI logic. Thus, it would not be surprising if, in a relatively short period, an AI with a postmodern mind frame emerges as a kind of humanist (and not transhumanist) response to this phenomenon, furthering us to return to the old but always reliable synapses of the neurons in our brains.

18

Reading from the edges:
Security for liquid risks

This has been one of my mantras, focus and simplicity.
The simple can be more difficult than the complex.
You have to work hard to make your thinking clean and make it simple,
but in the end, it's worth it because once you arrive
there, you can move mountains.

-Steve Jobs

Security is a system to manage risks and provide favorable environmental conditions so people, organizations, and societies can develop their potential. In the past, I have defined security as positive because its objective is not limited to keeping us free from threats but rather aims to build a world with more certainties. It seems, however, that the dynamics of the liquid world take us further away from spaces of certainty and predictability. Perhaps this defines a key challenge for security because it seems to have fallen behind in meeting its objectives while losing ground about accelerating risks. If the risks have changed in their morphology and nature, the goals of the security discipline must change. It should not only free us from threats but also return to spaces of greater certainty. This task may seem impossible to carry out in complex times.

Throughout these pages, I have tried to demonstrate the asymmetry with which risks advantage us. Evidence of this is that we have stopped understanding the world in which we live. This decoupling between security and risks is the liquid gap and the most critical challenge that we must address. To accomplish this task, we should not only change the set of rules with which we have been analyzing the problems. Hence, first of all, there is an urgent need to understand how complexity works.

But we are forced to go further since understanding is not enough. We must act assertively to function in environments that have become not only complex but also highly risky spaces. Various organizations were designed to operate in highly complex and dangerous environments. They are known as HROs (Highly Reliable Organizations). Some examples of HROs are air traffic systems, the control unit of a nuclear power plant, or NASA. In recent times and in the midst of accelerationism, many other organizations have entered, without noticing it, the High Complexity–High-Risk quadrant. They are being compromised in meeting their objectives since they were never prepared for environments with so much uncertainty and emerging threats. During the pandemic, hospitals had to become HROs. The countries that understood the moment moved in that direction, not only because they had to increase the resources available to face the successive waves of cases of the virus but also because a profound review of their processes and organizational culture was necessary to adapt to a new reality. It is worth understanding that most companies and organizations were not designed for liquid environments. Today, due to the changes we are experiencing, they will have to become HRO very soon. I am referring to organizations in multiple sectors, from supply and logistics chains to the food industry, the manufacturing of electronic microcomponents, telecommunications, protection service providers, and even police forces.

Security occupies a key and leading place in HROs because reliability is a factor directly proportional to it. An organization is trustworthy because it is secure. However, the security of the static and predictable will not make organizations highly reliable. Rather, the mindfulness of complexity will give a particular shape to leadership, structure, culture, and strategy to successfully deal with liquid risks. Reconceptualizing security so that it can respond effectively and thus generate spaces of certainty in response to the formation cycle of liquid risks requires addressing the following four axes interdependently:

- **Leadership:** Ability to understand complexity and produce changes to adapt the organization to the environment.

- **Structure:** Network of flows and connections on which the organization is supported to achieve its purposes.

- **Vision:** Clarity of objectives beyond uncertainty.

- **Culture:** It is referred to the collective consciousness around risk.

Creating and maintaining spaces of certainty will only be possible if we assume that security must act as a channel between, on one hand, a liquid and unpredictable world and, on the other, a zone of relative stability built from linear cause-effect relationships that further the projection of a near future. These stability zones will only be possible because, behind them, there will have to be a sustained security effort, with the ability to understand the complexity and establish the necessary networks with a collective awareness of the risk and clarity of objectives to overcome the uncertainty of the times. Thus, stability zones could be defined as multidimensional spaces where events typically unfold, pre-established rules do work, order, and security exist, and the immediate future is relatively easy to predict. In complex environments, stability zones are exceptional; although there may be many, everything will depend on the effort to sustain them. Between these stability zones and the complexity of the liquid world, there is a delimitation barrier called the normality line. It is a sort of protective envelope of stability and can be as tenuous or robust as the amount of risk awareness in the area. Normality could be interpreted as that which is within the norm. Normality encompasses those events that fall within the norm; in other words, it refers to all the events that occur without disturbing the certainties produced by everyday life. Even in very dynamic environments, some disruptions can be classified as usual because organizations can respond with agility to contain them within the zone of stability.

Stability zones are not isolated spaces of complexity, although there may be physical barriers that delimit them. These are, instead, areas where there is trust and certainty about environmental fluctuations. In some cases, these areas are more psychological constructs than actual structural spaces and depend more on order, culture, and compliance with rules than on more constraining physical elements. The organization's members' attitudes, skills, and culture differentiate stability zones from complex environments. As we pointed out, security is not extrinsic to the individual when we refer to the world of infinite possibilities. Still, it is rather a perception that has to be generated within him. Therefore, it is a security with full awareness of risks, a security for itself.

Figure 6
A model of security in highly complex and high-risk environments

In these more dynamic security models, rethought for environments of high complexity and high risks, we need to assume that within the stability zones coexist threats in latent states willing to act in the presence of favorable conditions. Such is the case of so-called domestic terrorism. It is fed by radicalized national individuals who have been exposed to powerful indoctrination networks, activating them to commit attacks in their areas of residence. That is why considering a border wall as a protection measure could be a deterrent against some migratory flows. However, they do not constitute true protective barriers against the power of liquid risks.

It would be bold on my part to affirm that liquid risks cannot be mitigated and that we are, therefore, forced to adapt and coexist with them. Eventually, we will develop capabilities and strategies to master them and perhaps neutralize them to render them harmless. However, we must understand that to reach the point of deactivation of liquid risks, the most extraordinary effort and investment will not be in infrastructure and technology but in transforming ourselves. Meanwhile, the challenge of managing these risks requires some guidelines aligned with the mentioned security model:

Leadership
Ability to understand complexity and turn this understanding into a tool
Ability to analyze the impacts of any decision that gives rise to new risks.
Lead the strategy and pay especial attention to details. Don't oversimplify
Ability to understand the process of production means and to foster new security tools based on individuals.
Ability to deal with uncertainty with flexibility.
Ability to convey certainties and manage uncertainty.

Table 2: Characteristics of the leadership in HRO

173

Structure

Ability to integrate the environment without undermining the security.

To have a flexible but conscious approach to adversity.

Development of skills to gather, analyze, and disseminate information.

An understanding of organizations as networks, ubiquitous but with no physical headquarters.

Ability to understand the world as pervaded by heterarchies, where relationships between individuals, organizations, and even societies privilege more flexible structures formed into networks instead of the classic pyramidal structures.

Ability to design flexible solutions able to deal with sudden or severe changes.

Table 3: Characteristics of the Structure in HRO

Vision

Daring to predict the future.

Envisioning the future in terms of scenarios.

Getting awareness of the increasing perishability of paradigms.

Confer a priority to the multiple above the singular, the difference above the similar, and the changing arrangements above the immutable systems. It is no longer sedentary but nomad, which is productive and sustains Foucault.

Facing risks without the fear of catastrophe (circumvent catastrophism).

Table 4: Characteristics of the Vision of the Future in HRO

Culture

Build an ample and in-depth awareness of liquid risks.

Develop skills for caution, self-control, and self-knowledge.

Develop relationships that can turn into partnerships in (forthcoming) times of adversity.

Learning to live according to a culture of protection: What is not lost is saved.

Take advantage of the cohesive power of organizational culture while the processes of individualization of the means of production advance.

Assume that complexity is a reality in a continuous imbalance. This imbalance produces gradients that lead everything to rise, aiming at stabilization. However, since so many varied forces are present, the system never reaches a resting position.

Table 5: Characteristics of the Vision of the Future in HRO

As we move into the 21st century, the world becomes increasingly complex. The instantaneousness of communications, the quantum leap of technologies, and discoveries in the fields of genetic engineering and green energies are contrasted with ideological-religious radicalisms, the crisis of representativeness of Western democracy, and the collapse of the fundamental values of coexistence in a world that does not stop its growth and accelerated consumption of resources.

In the complexity, new threats are interwoven with the fabric of reality that surfs the Dark Web, turning the frustration of young people into suicide bombs of great power, in the face of which security is almost nullified. For example, in 2020, according to the World Economic Forum risk report, cyber-mercenaries, almost without taking risks, obtained 406 million dollars in cryptocurrencies using ransomware. In 2017, a terrorist acting alone detonated himself with several kilos of explosives at the exit of a concert in the city of Manchester, in the United Kingdom, killing 22 people and injuring more than one hundred.

Contrary to intuition, the systems that have demonstrated the most resilience in managing complexity have integrated into their security the ability to interpret the environment by studying and identifying the phenomena surrounding them. Under this new paradigm, the protection of stability zones has migrated from a medieval castle model, where reality is isolated with a deep and dangerous moat to discourage potential enemies with intentions of penetrating and causing chaos, to a reality interconnected with its environment, highly specialized in the identification of threats, with the ability to forecast in the short term and prevent the materialization of risks through intelligence tools.

The acceleration of technology and globalization generates a gap separating knowledge societies from the rest of humanity, making adapting to change increasingly tricky. This acceleration translates into the loss of competitiveness of those who have stopped understanding the current reality and are outdated in their security models.

When returning to the ideas that motivated me to understand how we got here, it is essential to place ourselves in the context where new and complex forces shape the world, and failing to understand them makes us highly vulnerable. The acceleration of complexity has created a vacuum in the comprehension of reality, in which unprecedented dangers are brewing but have devastating impacts on all areas of life. The risks derived from the misunderstanding of the world act through forces that prioritize the temporary over the permanent, produce an addiction to accelerated change, and are marked by contradiction and uncertainty.

We must return to Zygmunt Bauman's thesis on *Modernity and the Liquid Society*, written more than three decades ago, which makes more sense today, at the beginning of the third millennium. Bauman wrote:

Reality has ceased to be a solid conglomerate, static, to become a fluid where everything changes at such an accelerated pace that it has erased the concept of what is permanent.

In the addiction to change, security, anchored in past paradigms, has been losing validity. Therefore, as we have pointed out, the time has come to start looking for answers in the future.

Liquid risks are the inevitable consequence of, on the one hand, the acceleration of complexity driven by technological development and globalization and, on the other, of society's inability to absorb and process the pace of change. It is in that gap of unconsciousness between the two that new and powerful threats thrive. A risk is liquid because its shape mutates and adapts to the environment that shapes it, it is difficult to contain, it spills easily, and although it is intangible when determined with some degree of precision, its effects are very real. These liquid risks have begun to manifest in multiple ways. They are no longer just about global terrorist organizations. Now, these forces move from political instability and the polarization of ideas to the horizontalization of power and the dizzying growth of alternative truths. However, they do not stop there. The new business areas of international organized crime, the more affordable power of AI, and the fragility of the reputations of people and organizations in the face of the attacks of social networks.

We have migrated from the firm, comfortable ground of certainties to the liquid swamps of uncertainty. The world has become less predictable with the acceleration of complexity and addiction to change. Linear cause-and-effect relationships have

177

disappeared while powerful new threats emerge. The greatest concern of current social and individual life is to prevent things from becoming fixed, so solid that they cannot be changed in the future. It is an aversion to what is permanent and, simultaneously, an addiction to change. These are times when nothing lasts long; new opportunities constantly appear that devalue existing ones, not only materially but also in relationships with others. A rapid dynamic of the temporal where the handles disappear, and the references fade away in short order.

We live in a liquid world, where everything flows, nothing is contained, and everything adapts to forms. Everything mutates, becoming intangible but with real consequences. In this liquid reality, full of liquid risks, we are close to losing the security paradigms. The construction of new references has become the most important challenge. Despite the prolonged reflection on the processes that give rise to liquid risks, several questions still remain to be answered. And I hope that accelerated time will possibly help us clarify them shortly:

At some point, will we begin to close the gap in liquid risks, or will we perhaps reach a point where we only generate certainty by applying algorithms developed by AI? Could the accelerated pace of change have some kind of limit imposed by the very frontiers of knowledge? To what extent can individuals and societies adapt to the demanding liquid environment, and can we do so before any of these new threats exploit some vulnerability at catastrophic levels and generate irreversible changes? We are only beginning to connect the dots and discover some patterns, but we are still far from fully understanding the nature of such risks, and mitigating their effects remains an immense challenge.

I have reflected on the convenience of analyzing the risks that impact our present when immersed in them and surrounded by complexity and uncertainty. I have spent months searching for answers within the folds of recent history and the paths that begin to demarcate the future. Because we are in moments of greatest doubt, urgent needs arise to understand. Sometimes, amid the blackest darkness, the small flame of a candle can illuminate enough to know where we are and ensure that the first steps are not taken falsely. I cannot write from the wise rest that time confers. I dare say I am doing it from the uncontrollable anguish of all those seeking some certainty. Therefore, there is an urgent need to invert the paradigm of the human being as an object of security and transform it into a subject. I know this is a complicated discussion if we consider the significant threats that arrive just when the individual is more vulnerable. Still, I deem it to be necessary if we aspire to build natural defenses against liquid risks.

19

Security and freedom

By wanting freedom, we discover that it depends entirely on the freedom of others.

-Jean Paul Sartre

Every level of security involves a transaction. Something must be surrendered to move to a higher state of tranquility and certainty. Security, therefore, has a cost that is usually measured in terms of money, time, comfort, effort, and, in classical terms, freedom. However, in its broadest conception, security contains a fundamental objective: reducing causes that prevent human beings from fully exercising their rights. In this sense, it operates as an active promoter of the life and well-being of citizens. Frederick Hayek, in his work, *New Studies in Philosophy, Politics, Economics and the History of Ideas*, argues that when societies are allowed to self-organize in their economy, a spontaneous order emerges that is the product of human action and not of design, which makes these societies more accessible and equitable. Such a spontaneous order is what led to complex systems. Complex systems were also the idea that, in 1984, led several scientists who had fled the Manhattan Project to found the Santa Fe Institute in New Mexico. There, they would develop in-depth what was later called the sciences of complexity, a discipline drawing from the open systems theory, open systems as a basis, such as economics, communities of living beings, cellular biology, and quantum physics. Over the years, dozens of important scientists visited the cloisters of the institute. Murray Gell-Mann, 1969 Nobel Prize in Physics; John Henry Holland, father of the genetic algorithm; and Stuart Alan Kauffman, developer of the thesis on biological complexity, were some of those distinguished visitors. I have found the notion of the spontaneous order of the economy challenging because, in some way, security in a world of infinite possibilities can become a powerful system for freedom instead of its antagonist. Although I am not comparing economics with security, the former, when left free, becomes complex, and the latter, when ordered with an understanding of complexity, becomes an instrument to empower societies, which is an exercise of freedom. So, both are sensitive to power and are frequently manipulated to control or repress, not only in totalitarian regimes but also in democracies. Thus, in the name of biosecurity during the COVID-19 pandemic, tough regulations against Western Europe, Canada, Australia, and New Zealand populations were implemented. More often than not, those regulations transcended the health sector and extended their scope to the police sector.

The acceleration of complexity led to the collapse of what, in the recent past, had been the Paradigm of the solid state. Thus, many of the references making up the pillars of societies were erased. This, in turn, led to a relativization of society that had, amongst its many consequences, a subordination of liberty in the name of security. So, the classic cycle of totalitarian control was defined and designed. Considered this way, security takes the form of an adhesive, a thin layer that sticks to the surface of society and its individuals to protect them from threats. However, if the environment in which it is embedded is not understood, the State will have to shield its fragility in order not to be attacked by the unknown. In the narrative of the weak society that needs to be protected by the sheltering

182

State, it is right here where the temptation of power over freedom emerges. Therefore, there is an urgent need to invert the paradigm of the human being as an object of security and transform her into a subject, which is undoubtedly a complicated discussion considering the significant threats that arrive just at the moment in which the individual is more vulnerable, but necessary if we aspire to build natural defenses against liquid risks.

Security, like so many other conditions for sustaining civilized life, will have to go through a review process to make it suitable to understand, deal with, and tame and shape the accelerated globalizing dynamic. On the other hand, both the risk analyst and the individual will have to approach and merge with reality, no matter how much uncertainty such an experience may bring them. Empowered by such a new and contemporary vision of security, they will be more likely to become fully aware of the liquid quality of the world. This new vision of the world's nature will likely place them in better conditions to take on the challenges of freedom from a less restrictive position. On the social, economic, and environmental levels, it is similar to what the United Nations Development Program (UNDP) defined in 1994 as *human security*. This concept underlines the right of people to live in freedom and dignity, free from poverty and despair, as well as to have equal opportunities to fully develop their human potential. It is a more effective and focused multidimensional structure that combines peace, security, and the exercise of human rights in a new development paradigm. Additionally, we cannot ignore that a citizen immersed in a context of violence, unable to meet their basic needs or primary health care, simply does not have the capacity to calibrate the weight that security could have on freedom. Hence, in addition to being a guarantee, human security is a right inherent to the person, so it cannot pretend to compete with other inalienable rights such as freedom.

Although nations continue to concentrate their security efforts on maintaining peace as an essential element for stability and coexistence, the potential for threats quickly shifting to the liquid state cannot be ignored. Extreme poverty, forced migrations, climate change, global economic crisis, and global financial crises reveal a vulnerability associated with rapidly spreading risks. And this process takes place even faster in nations with institutional weaknesses. This is the case in many countries in South America and nearly all the countries in Africa, countries undergoing the natural, political, economic, and social shocks of a world that seems to move abruptly. It would be worth remembering today the warning made in 2017 by the American general:

We have entered a world we believed we were prepared to live in. However, we now realize that we arrogantly ignore almost everything about it. One thing we ignore about this world is the nature and dimension of the threats approaching us.

Perhaps time is too short to build a robust truth, although it may be long enough to gather information and analyze the trends. This is why I am convinced we have crossed a threshold and entered a new world radically different from the one we used to abode. A world that dazzles us because of an increasing diversity of uncertainties that we keep on examining with ancient magnifying glasses outperformed microscopes and telescopes that are unable to assist us in the discovery of the hidden reality of this accelerated world whose very nature scares us up to the point of self-deception.

When the narrative alluringly persuades us of freedom because we are in the era of plug and play and, at the same time, we are confronted with the accelerated complexity of a liquid world, we realize that the security paradigm designed for a static and solid world is useless. This paradigm will remain useless no matter how many multiverses of infinite possibilities there are, AI-empowered smartphones or whichever new devices may be developed and offered to us in the future. No technological innovation will lead us to the awareness of the liquid world because it is our responsibility to create such an awareness from scratch with a sense of urgency.

Once we acknowledge that we live in an increasingly complex world, security will have to turn the simple into a value. We need to fully awaken to the idea that in the world to come, we will have to sculpt certainties out of the territories of uncertainty. We will also have to learn to forecast out of the unpredictability of times. But instead of accomplishing this task assuming the linearity of calm, we would do it from the turbulence of the emergency. However we see it, we have become nomads on the same terrain where we were once sedentary and free. So, as final words, I only have to remember Soren Kierkegaard: *Without risk, there is no faith.*

Epilogue

Now that you have reached the end of the book, you may be asking yourself: what can I do to avoid or mitigate the liquid risks? Is such a thing possible, or am I rather condemned to live with these risks in a permanent state of mobile adaptation? The answers to these two questions may be more philosophical than practical. We could appeal to the well-known phrase about knowledge as a form of liberation, which translates into developing awareness about the nature and logic of the liquid. Thus, we accept that these risks are now ingrained in and have made themselves part of the fabric of reality. So, whether we like it or not, we cannot rid ourselves of them. However, after several years of working on the subject, I am convinced that a dimension of liquid risks can be brought to the practical level. In order to approach it, we first need to understand in depth how these risks work and ground the concepts in models that can be implemented by individuals, families, societies, companies, and even states.

Some readers of the Spanish version told me that they ended up reading the book with a sense of powerlessness in the face of a world that is no longer inviting to be understood, much less to be controlled by human beings. If that were the case, any mitigation effort would be useless because I am arguing liquid risks are now an integral part of the world and its complex dynamics. However, I never intended to convey such a sense of inutility of action regarding liquid risks revolving around us. In order to start dealing with liquid risks, we must develop strategies, and policies that consider the fact that these risks are an outcome of complexity. They would be an emerging property of the new level of high complexity and accelerated rate of change we live in. So, we cannot generate simple solutions or practical survival recipes to overcoming them as if they were a turbulence of reality that would dissipate, returning afterward to times of certainty. With this idea in mind and on the path to identifying the practical dimension of the liquid world, I will demarcate three territories: the mental-cultural, the strategic deployed on the ground, and a territory that is a fusion of the previous two.

The Liquid Mindset

Both the Pre Socratic philosopher Heraclitus (540 BC - 480 BC) and the German philosopher Friedrich Nietzsche (1844 – 1900) were two of the main precursors of ideas about reality as a space in motion. In the 20th century, these ideas were further developed and updated by Zygmunt Bauman in his book Liquid Modernity (1999). Heraclitus and Nietzsche share a vision of the world as a constant flow of change and becoming. Heraclitus is known for his famous phrase: You cannot step twice into the same rivers, for fresh waters are ever flowing in upon you. In this fragment, the philosopher refers to the ever-changing nature of everything. This idea of perpetual flux and the impermanence of all that exists resonated deeply with Nietzsche, who saw the world as a dance of forces in constant transformation. Both thinkers rejected the notion of absolute and immutable truths, embracing a dynamic perspective of reality. A dynamism that, in this book, we have designated as liquid. Since we are unprepared to live in a world in constant change and becoming, we seek to conceive of ourselves as entities with a transcendent purpose that generates the illusion that we are treading on solid ground, capable of resisting a continuous becoming. For Nietzsche and later for Bauman, Western philosophy has placed fictitious references before us to give the appearance that we are developing in the solidity of reason when, actually, everything flows, including ourselves, in an unstoppable current. We could argue that the veil covering the true nature of reality in permanent change was starting to be removed by technological accelerationism and its derived complexity. A reality that we do not fully understand because we remain tied to fixed references that lose all their value in the constant becoming. The first major challenge is, therefore, to shift the mindset from the immovable to the liquid. Only those individuals, organizations, and societies capable of removing references will achieve that transition and get the possibility of understanding reality. They will begin to decode strategies to contain or mitigate liquid risks. This process involves multiple changes in practice, from principles and values, organizational culture, forms of association, and business models to the relationship between the state and its citizens.

Organizations and societies must decide how to navigate in this new context. It's not about challenging the previous model but about opening up to new possibilities. It might seem contradictory that we are encouraged to reduce aversion to risk in a liquid world. However, it is not about taking more risks but rather about learning to assume risks with full awareness of their nature and under the assumption that stability or a sense of permanence are no longer valid values. Hence, the focus shifts from the transcendental to the situational, from defined boundaries to blurred and gray areas, and in the process, power gets reordered under heterarchical and decentralized structures. As Nietzsche would frame it, transitioning from apparent solidity to constant becoming is not a simple or painless evolution. But in the long run, it will be unavoidable to seize the opportunities of these liquid times that have come to stay.

The liquid strategy

While a new mindset is indispensable to face the liquid world, successfully navigating through it requires a strategic framework that enables organizations to assemble an agile and highly adaptive structure, defined primarily by two main axes: a nonlinear view of reality and the capacity for decentralized self-organization. Nonlinearity refers to processes where the relationships between causes and effects are not necessarily proportional, direct, or evident, so understanding them requires a more detailed analysis of changes. A liquid strategy cannot settle for the obvious and needs to delve into its design and execution. Nonlinearity implies recognizing the complexity and interconnection of emerging phenomena, as well as understanding that small changes can generate significant impacts on outcomes. The liquid strategic vision acknowledges that the results or properties of reality can arise unpredictably from the interaction of its components. These emergent properties are usually difficult to predict if we rely only on observing individual components, making an anticipatory model for understanding reality indispensable.

On the other hand, complexity does not respond to imposed or highly hierarchical structuring patterns. It operates with spontaneous schemes in which the interaction among the system's components self-organizes without needing external direction. In liquid times, companies must be able to flow with environmental variations, enhancing themselves by forming agile and temporary strategic alliances and partnerships in the convergence process based on agendas or interests. This allows them to seize emerging opportunities and adapt to changing circumstances.

At this point, I would like to make a philosophical crossover to formulate a liquid strategy. The Danish philosopher Soren Kierkegaard (1813 - 1855) argued that we cannot access reality exclusively through reason. He stated that we need to experience the environment existentially, meaning that we have to live reality individually in all its complexity in order to decode the world. Understanding reality (and truth) will be a subjective and particular process for each individual, adapted to their circumstances in entire interaction with their environment. Therefore, there will be no identical strategies, as organizations must undergo the experience of existing in their reality as an indispensable component to chart a course of action.

Formulating strategies for the liquid world cannot happen in an isolated laboratory environment, with complete control of variables. On the contrary, a liquid strategy is adaptive and begins with identifying initial conditions. Organizations need to exist in their own reality to capitalize on the opportunities offered by emerging phenomena, which, being unpredictable, should be managed with great agility. Strategic planning becomes a process of becoming, understood as the process or state of change that occurs in time and space.

The liquid game

On the pages of this book, I have been leaving clues on how to play in the liquid context. I think that at some point, we have to take action, and it is precisely here, in the two-way game between adaptation and creation, that we can practice that fusion of mindset with strategy. I will list a decalogue of actions that are characteristic of what I call the liquid game. When playing this game, some actions will be more accessible or more applicable than others. My purpose is to give both practitioners and risk managers input so that they can begin to formulate a blueprint of action plans to manage liquid risks in organizations and society. These initiatives do not have a specific order of execution, and, as a whole, they can be seen as a choreography of adaptation and creation.

Embrace change and uncertainty
Accept and embrace change and uncertainty as constant and inevitable forces. Organizations must prepare for fluidity and continuous transformation. Implicit in this acceptance is the flexibility of thought, agility, and adaptability in decision-making, as well as an anticipatory attitude towards environmental changes.

Understand complexity
While there is no single recipe for understanding complexity, a good start is identifying the forces or variables operating in the reality surrounding us and determining their current state. Navigating complexity is part of a continuous process of building organizational resilience.

191

Culture of risk tolerance
Organizations must recognize that uncertainty implies risks but also opportunities. A key to shaping a risk culture is encouraging work teams to take calculated risks and experiment without fear of failure. Celebrate attempts, even if they are not successful, and use failures as learning opportunities. This is the basis of resilience.

Lead by example
In the face of uncertainty, leading people through example is the most powerful way a leader can influence their organization. When leaders consistently model the behaviors and values they preach, they inspire genuine trust and respect in their teams. They are not simply dictating rules but demonstrating what they consider essential through their actions. The classic image of the leader above their followers has migrated to a more horizontal and direct model that also adds a component of humility in the face of the unknown.

Innovate
Innovation is an integral part of the production process and not an add-on that operates separately or in isolation from the corporate reality and its challenges. Ideas must be generated at all levels of the organization to innovate. A powerful exercise to encourage innovation begins with interdisciplinary collaboration and creating an environment where new and different initiatives are valued in safe spaces that foster the free expression of ideas without judgments or criticism.

Continuous learning
Learning is an endless game in the liquid world. Organizations that understand the game can insert it into their culture and connect it to innovation, making their customers part of the process. Provide training and professional development opportunities for your employees to acquire new skills and knowledge. This will allow them to more easily adapt to changes and contribute to creating new solutions. Learning is a way of becoming.

Build networks
Self-organization emerges from complexity because it is the most efficient way to coordinate in the face of environmental challenges. These organizational models are expressed in constructing networks that intertwine and through which information, modes of behavior, and responses propagate. Organizations must become nodes of these networks and constantly interact with their environment. Networks empower teams and individuals to respond agilely to changes in reality. In a non-linear environment, centralized and hierarchical decision-making can be too slow and rigid, so networks provide autonomy and decentralize the ability to act without losing alignment.

Develop a purpose and its narrative
Communications in the liquid world require defining a shared purpose, which provides a general sense of direction without being tied to rigid plans. This purpose must be accompanied by narratives that present it appropriately to the organization. This creates a strategic, emotional, and cultural anchor point that allows fluidity and adaptation within a shared values and goals framework. The purpose is more than a goal or objective. It is a commitment rooted in the team's identity. The general sense of direction transcends specific circumstances and operational details. Instead of limiting creativity and adaptability, purpose acts as a catalyst for innovation and positive change. Individuals find a sense of belonging and connection by aligning around this shared purpose.

Continuous review and optimization
Organizations must remain agile and adaptable in the liquid world. Processes are, by definition, the moving parts of the system, so they cannot remain invariable when reality is changing. The key to processes is to ensure they stay relevant, which implies regularly analyzing workflows, identifying if there is a saturation of tasks in specific nodes, eliminating redundant steps, and adopting technologies or methods to improve productivity. The culture of

improvement is part of the organizational liquid mindset. All levels of the organization are empowered to challenge the status quo and make proposals to optimize processes.

Leverage the Power of Technology

Technology is the empowering expression of reality. The accelerationism that characterizes liquid times can be measured through technological change. Not taking advantage of that power would be a contradiction since the threats acting in the environment constantly use it. In the liquid context, technology is a tool for anticipation, intelligence data, and information analysis, and not an end in itself. The key is that it operates on demand. It must be considered as a high availability and security service. Technology must also facilitate organizational adaptation and resilience processes.

The Eternal Recurrence

To conclude, I would like to go back to Nietzsche and his idea of eternal recurrence. It is mentioned in several of his works but is laid out in detail in The Gay Science and Thus Spoke Zarathustra. According to Nietzsche, the universe comprises a finite amount of matter and energy. If we assume that the universe is infinite in time, then all possible configurations of that finite matter and energy will have to repeat themselves over and over again, eternally. This means that every event, every situation, every detail of our lives has occurred identically before and will occur an infinite number of times in the future. Although this idea may seem contradictory in the liquid world described by Bauman, where the only constant is accelerated change, there is a profound connection between these two seemingly opposed concepts. The liquid world is characterized by the dissolution of the permanent, the fluidity of structures, and the transience of forms. Nothing is perpetual or stable; everything flows and constantly transforms.

Paradoxically, Nietzsche's idea of the eternal return provides a valuable perspective for coping with the anguish of constant flux. If we accept that everything will happen repeatedly, and despite becoming, there will always be a new and unique opportunity because it will not occur in the same environment or under the same conditions. Hence, each decision and each action acquires transcendental importance. Each moment is an opportunity to shape a future that will inevitably repeat itself. Instead of resisting change, we must learn to flow with it, to anticipate and take advantage of constant transformations. We have no choice but to cultivate a liquid mindset of continuous learning, experimentation, and creation, knowing that each cycle will bring new lessons and opportunities.

The eternal return places us in such a way that our actions and decisions have consequences that extend beyond the present. An awareness of the impact we have on reality is essential, and there will be repercussions that will propagate through the cycles to come. In a liquid reality fraught with risks, where uncertainty and complexity are the norm, the idea of an eternal return can be an invaluable compass. Let us embrace change, learn from every experience, and make decisions with a long-term perspective, recognizing that our actions will have consequences that will repeat eternally. Those who incorporate this vision will be better prepared to navigate the turbulent waters of the liquid world and emerge strengthened with each cycle. Beyond the impermanence, everything we do matters and is valuable and necessary for that instant in time.

About the author

Alberto Ray, born in Venezuela in 1967, is an Electronics Engineer specializing in strategic risk analysis and decision-making in complex scenarios with over three decades of work experience. He is the CEO of Smart Risk Consulting, a United States-based organization focused on analyzing emerging risks. Alberto has been a security consultant for companies, governments, and institutions in many South American countries and has a Diploma in Coexistence and Citizen Safety. He is a co-author of the MAPS21 Model, a comprehensive security risk management method. Over his career as a consultant, he has given talks and been a keynote speaker at multiple security seminars and conferences in Venezuela, Latin America, the United States, and Europe. Ray is the founder of the Security Thinking Center: The Risk Awareness Council (TRAC), and his publications include MAPS Navigation Chart for a Secure Organization (2014), RAY in Security, A Simple Look at a Complex World (2016), and MAPS21 (2021). Alberto publishes weekly pieces on various issues related to the subject of the present book on his blog, AlbertoRay.com. Since 2019, Alberto has lived in Florida with his wife, two children, and Penelope, the wisest Yorki.

Further Readings

- Thinking in Systems. Donella H. Meadows. Chelsea Green Publishing. 2008

- The Filter Bubble. Eli Pariser. Penguin Group. 2011

- Thank You for Being Late. Thomas L. Friedman. Picador. 2016

- Team of Teams. Stanley McChrystal. Penguin Group. 2015

- Risk Society: Towards a New Modernity. Ulrick Beck. SAGE Publications Ltd. 1992

- Liquid Modernity. Zygmunt Bauman. Polity. 2000

- On Complexity. Edgar Morin. Hampton Press 2008

- Chaos Under Heaven. Josh Rogin. Houghton Mifflin Hartcourt Publishing 2021

- World Without Mind. Franklin Foer. Penguin Random House 2017

- Skin in the Game. Nassim Nicholas Taleb. Random House 2018

- Retrotopia. Zygmunt Bauman. Polity 2017

- Risk. Stanley McChrystal. Editorial Portfolio. 2021

- The Globotics Upheaval. Richard Baldwin. Oxford University Press 2019

- The Quark and the Jaguar. Murray Gell-Mann. Henry Holt Publishers. 1994

- Twilight of Democracy. Anne Applebaum. Anchor Books 2021

- Predictability Irrational. Dan Ariely. Harper Collins Publishers 2009

- The Infinite Game. Simon Sinek. Portfolio/Penguin 2019

- Assad, or we burn the county. Sam Dagher. Little, Brown Company 2019

- The Moral Landscape. Sam Harris. Free Press 2010

- Time Reborn. Lee Smolin. First Mariner Books 2014

- Thinking in Bets. Annie Duke. Portfolio/Penguin 2019

- The Coming Wave. Mustafa Suleyman. Crown Publishing. 2023

- Superintelligence. Nick Bostrom. Oxford University Press. 2014

- Simulacra and Simulation. Jean Baudrillard. Michigan Press. 1994

- The Burnout Society. Byung - Chul Han. Stanford Briefs. 2015

- Discipline and punish. Michel Foucault. Vintage Books. 1995

- On the Genealogy of Morals. Friedrich Nietzsche. Penguin Classics. 2014

References

Prologue

1.Beck accurately define three of the major characteristics. Ulrick Beck, Risk Society, Towards a New Modernity, London: SAGE, 1992. xiv

2.In a lucid essay written in 1972, Gregory Bateson. Steps to an Ecology of Mind: Collected Essays in Anthropology, Psychiatry, Evolution, and Epistemology. Chandler Publishing Company. xviii

3.In 1984, the philosopher Han Jonas, in his essential work. The Imperative of Responsibility: In Search of an Ethics for the Technological Age, Chicago: University of Chicago Press, 1979. xviii

Introduction

4.The WHO declaration of the COVID-19 pandemic": https://www.who.int/europe/emergencies/situations/covid-19 2

Danger: There are no borders

5.The fact is that global warming and infectious diseases.scientists have found evidence that in the last 100 million of years global temperatures had spiked that could be defined as Global Warming. One was the Cretaceous Hot Greenhouse "roughly 92 million years ago, about 25 million years before Earth's last dinosaurs went extinct. Widespread volcanic activity may have boosted atmospheric carbon dioxide. For more on this see: https://www.climate.gov/news-features/climate-qa/whats-hottest-earths-ever-been. This evidence does not disprove the scientific evidence that sustains humans responsibility in the current warming of the planet...7

6.In his book Risk Society (1992). Ulrick Beck, Risk Society, Towards a New Modernity, London: SAGE Publications..8

204

Futurists of the present wanted

We come from chaos, and towards chaos, we go

Walking the tightrope of complexity

Hansel and Gretel with algorithms

Multiplexed in a nudist beach

Productivity is now nomadic

The blood that feeds the system

The kingdom of the heterarchical

54.In the latter's case, it overcame. https://insightcrime.org/mexico-organized-crime-news/sinaloa-cartel-profile/. 110

55.Antifragility is a neologism coined by the Lebanese-born mathematician Nassim Nicholas Taleb. Antifragile, New York: Random House, 2014. 111

56.In the volatile world of liquid modernity. Ibidem, p.9 112

Liquid elections or how to hack the system

57.For example, in the 2019 Bolivian elections. For an independent appraisal of the 2019 Bolivian elections see the report (in Spanish): "Análisis de Integridad Electoral, Elecciones Generales en el Estado Plurinacional de Bolivia", Secretaría para el Fortalecimiento de la Democracia (SFD)/ Departamento para la Cooperación y Observación Electoral (DECO), 21 October, 2019. 119

58.In the 2017 elections for the National Constituent Assembly, Smartmatic. See (in Spanish): "Declaración de Smartmatic sobre la reciente elección de la Asamblea Constituyente en Venezuela", August, 2017.https://www.smartmatic.com/es/noticias/declaracion-de-smartmatic-sobre-la-reciente-eleccion-de-la-asamblea-constituyente-en-venezuela/ 119

59.In 2020, when the peak of electoral liquefaction in the United States. Ibidem p. 20.. 120

60.On the other hand, each state has several modalities for early voting. https://www.pewresearch.org/politics/2020/11/20/the -voting experience-in-2020/. 120

61.In 1981, Samuel Huntington predicted. American Politics, The Promise of Disharmony, Cambridge: Harvard University Press, 1981. 122

62.David Brooks, a well-known NYT editorialist. See Brooks's essay in The Atlantic, published on October 5, 2020: "America Is Having a Moral Convulsion." 123

Liquid totalitarianism

63.An investigation published by The Economist Intelligence Unit. See: A Report by EIU, Democracy Index 2021: the China challenge", 2021.https://www.eiu.com/n/campaigns/democracy-index-2021/................................ 127

64.What Fukuyama called The End of History. Francis Fukuyama, The End of History and the Last Man, New York, Free Press, 1992.........................128

65.The horrific events of September 2001. For The Global War on Terror, see: https://www.georgewbushlibrary.gov/research/topic-guides/global-war-terror, For a critical examination of the war on Terror see: Ivo H. Daalder and James M. Lindsay, Nasty, Brutish and Long: America's War on Terrorism, Brookings, December 2001. https://www.brookings.edu/articles/nasty-brutish-and-long-americas-war-on-terrorism/..............128

66.Early efforts toward breaking the Principle of Alternation in Power. For an examination of the use of this referendum to strengthen the authoritarian government to power see: Bernard Gwertzman Interviewing Allan Brewer Carias, in "Referendum in Venezuela Hardens Chavez's 'Authoritarian Regime', Council on Foreign Relations, February 17, 2009.. 129

67.A similar process was furthered by Evo Morales in Bolivia............... 129

68.Thus, in George Orwell's novel 1984, the Party manipulates language. For more on this see: Blakemore, S (1984) "Language and Ideology in Orwell's 1984", Social Theory and Practice, 10, No. 3, A Special Issue: Orwell's 1984 (Fall 1984), pp. 349-356 (8 pages), Published By: Florida State University Department of Philosophy. 131

69.Al Assad was prepared as the successor in 1996. https://es.wikipedia.org/wiki/H%C3%A1fez_al-%C3%81sad... 133

70.In the revealing book about the Syrian civil war. Sam Dagher. Assad or we burn the country, How One Family's Lust for Power Destroyed Syria. Little, Brown Company 2019.. 133

71.In May 2021, Bashar was voted. https://www.dw.com/en/syria-election-results-bashar-assad-wins-4th- term/a-57695 134

72.https://www.weforum.org/reports/global-risks-report-2022........ 134

From The Matrix to liquid wars

73.Today, ideology has mutated into more liquid forms. For a discussion of the intricate relationship between power, language and discourse in Gramsci, see his work The Prison Notebooks. There he developed his theory of hegemony, which would be collectively built by the ruling class not by coercion but by a consent that is reached through language. In the present times of digital social networks, those ruling the discourse and, therefore building the hegemony, would be the owners of the big tech companies. As Mustafa Suleyman argues in The Coming Wave (2023), the big tech corporations, specially those who lead the development of AI, will soon be more powerful than nation states.for a discussion of narratives as a soft power, see: Jason P. Lowery's book: Softwar: A Novel Theory on Power Projection and the National Strategic Significance of Bitcoin. 138

74.In May 2023, Pope Francis warned of the risk of "self-destruction" of humanity. See: El Clarín May 5, 2023. 142

75.For example, the UK Counter Terrorism Internet Referral Unit. https://wiki.openrightsgroup.org/wiki/Counter-Terrorism_Internet_ Referral_Unit. 143

76.Some authors have used the term to describe a type of confrontation. On the concept of liquid wars see: Max Mutschler & Marius Bales, "Liquid or Solid Warfare? Autocratic States, Non-State Armed Groups and the Socio-Spatial Dimension of Warfare in Yemen", Geopolitics, Volume 29, 2024. 143

Catastrophism: The vector of intimidation

77.Of the first five risks with the highest probabilities and impacts. https:// www.weforum.org/reports/global-risks-report-2022. 151

78.To do this, it is helpful to take Robert S. Kaplan and Anette Mikes'classification of risks. See: Robert S. Kaplan and Anette Mikes. Managing Risks: A New Framework. Harvard Business Review. June 2012. https://hbr.org/2012/06/managing-risks-a-new- framework. 151

Living with an artificial alien

79.I take the ideas from Mustafa Suleyman, a British researcher and founder of DeepMind. On March 19, 2024, Microsoft's CEO Satya Nadella announced that Mustafa Suleyman had been appointed CEO and EVP of Microsoft AI, a newly created unit "focused on advancing Copilot and our other consumer AI products and research. 157

80.Suleyman argues in his book The Coming Wave. Mustafa Suleyman with Michael Bhaskar, The Coming Wave, Technology, Power and the 21st Century's Greatest Dilemma, New York, Crown, 2023. 157

Epilogue

Index

Brexit 52, 54.

bubbles 76, 78, 79, 91, 164, 209.

C

Cambridge Analytica xxvi, 54.

Catastrofismo 137, 149, 150, 151, 152, 153, 174.

Chávez, Hugo 129.

Chernobyl 8.

China 42, 43, 120, 207, 208, 211.

Chinese Communist Party 34, 115.

CNN 103.

Colombia 70, 72, 110.

complexity ix, xiv, xv, xvi, xvii, xix, xx, xxi, xxv, 3, 4, 10, 12, 15, 17, 19, 20, 31, 34, 35, 42, 45, 50, 53, 57, 58, 59, 65, 66, 67, 68, 69, 70, 71, 72, 75, 78, 79, 80, 84, 95, 96, 97, 98, 114, 115, 116, 120, 123, 130, 142, 143, 147, 150, 153, 156, 157, 161, 165, 170, 171, 172, 173, 175, 176, 177, 179, 181, 182, 184, 188, 189, 190, 191, 192, 193, 195, 206, 208.

complex thinking vii, 75, 209.

compliance 41, 172.

containment 158, 161, 162, 166, 167.

COVID-19 2, 36, 43, 54, 75, 83, 98, 162, 182, 205.

crime xvi, xxii, 31, 32, 49, 51, 53, 71, 77, 90, 106, 109, 110, 115, 130, 177, 210.

cryptocurrency 41, 42, 207, 208.

D

Dagher, Sam 133, 202, 212.

Dark Web 1, 31, 175.

Deep Learning 76.

Deleuze, Gilles 96, 210.

E

ecological risks 8.

elites 52, 76.

Escobar, Pablo 110, 210.

Eternal Recurrence 194.

Ethereum 41, 208.

Europe 48, 54, 110, 134, 182, 197.

Evergreen 43, 208.

F

fake news 21, 30, 43, 77.

Fox 103, 207.

Friedman, Thomas 22, 75, 201, 207.

Fukushima 40.

G

generative AI 155.

Germany 52, 72, 208.

global warming 7, 150, 205.

gray zones xvi, 32, 77.

Guzmán, El Chapo 110.

H

I

K

L

Acknowledgments

This book had several previous stages before I began writing it. I made that first approach in Venezuela, and Marisol Fuentes built a schedule of fascinating interviews that served as a warm-up. From those conversations, I especially remember Ramón Piñango, Benigno Alarcón, José Toro Hardy, and very particularly Víctor Guedez, who had read almost all of Zygmunt Bauman's published books. To all of them, my gratitude for those first lights.

In a second move, after two years, I shared an initial draft with several friends who read it and generously shared their opinions. I thank them all for their time and dedication. I must point out Vladimir Tovar, Morella Behrens and Jorge Barrios.

In the final stage of the Spanish version of Liquid Risks, Florantonia Singer intervened, to whom I am especially grateful. In the midst of our revision work, she faced a significant challenge, a serious car accident. Despite this, she remained dedicated, patiently reading and revising my texts and offering her insights when I was unsure how to conclude the text. Her resilience and commitment are truly commendable.

In this same final phase, I asked my great friend, Luis Emilio Bruni, to thoroughly read the manuscript, make the comments that he considered pertinent, and go further and write the book's prologue. I know that his work was impeccable and helped me better define several concepts that appear throughout the reading, all this during a thousand obligations that academic life demands of him. I know he did it with the greatest pleasure. I am very grateful to Luis, and I hope that in the future, we can write an essay together about one of the subjects of this book.

I must thank Lorenzo Dávalos, another great friend and exceptional human being, for making possible this English edition of Liquid Risks. He worked hard not only to translate the book but also to be the true editor of the final text. His advice and insight have notably improved the quality and content of the book. I eagerly look forward to our future collaborations, as I believe Lorenzo's role as a Copilot of the project will be invaluable.

Finally, I sincerely thank my son Alejandro Carlos, who dared to lay out the book and shape it to turn it into something readable. I cannot conclude without expressing my appreciation to my wife, María Eugenia, who, for years and with great patience, has listened to me talk about a thousand crazy things, including this topic of liquid risks.

www.ingramcontent.com/pod-product-compliance
Lightning Source LLC
Chambersburg PA
CBHW070813270326
41927CB00010B/2402

9 7 9 8 2 1 8 4 4 8 3 8 7